2

THE POWER OF THE BODY IN LEADERSHIP

THE POWER OF THE BODY
IN LEADERSHIP

The body is your raft for traveling the sea of life.[1] *Chinese Proverb*

I once struggled with neck and shoulder pain and went to various medical doctors who treated my bones, muscles, and nervous system without satisfactory relief. During a business trip to China, I greatly benefited from a Chinese medicine doctor who not only eased my pain, but also taught me that we cannot treat our skeletal structure, muscular structure, and our nervous system as separate systems. The inspiration for me is that, in leadership, we cannot separate our Mind (thoughts, beliefs, perspectives, mindset) from the Body (feelings, sensations, actions, spoken words).

In our modern world, particularly in the West, leadership has traditionally been associated with our Mind only – cognitive abilities and rational thinking. Our Body is often viewed as merely a vehicle to carry our head from meeting to meeting. More recently, we have learned that our Body carries the memory of our repeated patterns of thinking, emotions, and behaviors. Most of our daily decisions are not intentionally made by our conscious Mind, they are executed automatically by our Body instead. Based on latest learning by neuroscientists, more than 95% of our behavior is the result of unconscious patterns with little or no conscious awareness on our part."[2]

We are whole as human beings. Mind and Body are inextricably inter-connected, we cannot separate the two in leadership.

In real life, however, we are far behind on incorporating the wholeness of the Mind and Body into leadership development, behavior changes, and coaching others.

As high-performing leaders, we help others and teams perform at their best. Increasing leadership capacity involves positive leadership behavior change. Driving positive leadership behavior change involves two things: awareness and action. Awareness is part of our BEING, our "inner game", or how we choose to be. Actions are part of our DOING, our "outer game", or what we choose to do.

In supporting leaders to achieve powerful results, working with our Body and Mind deepens awareness and accelerates actions, elevates both our "inner game" and "outer game" to achieve sustainable growth, and helps unlock a brand new level of possibilities. I call this Embodied Leadership, a leadership approach that actively integrates the holistic intelligence of the Body and Mind to increase leadership effectiveness.

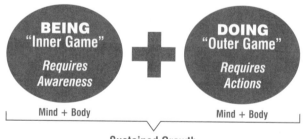

Working with our Full Body and our Whole-Self

BEING

BEING is how we master our relationship with the inner world, or how we play the "inner game". It is how we choose to be. This includes how we choose to see ourselves and the world; how we manage our physical, emotional, and mental states as we exist in the world. This precedes and drives our actions – our DOING.

To lead others, we first need to know ourselves and master ourselves. Leadership starts with us and it starts from within – our BEING.

Playing the "inner game" and accessing our state of BEING requires emotional intelligence and insightful self-awareness. There is a significant difference between knowing something conceptually and really feeling and sensing something intimately.

Award-winning researcher ad professor Alan Fogel points out two different kinds of self-awareness: Conceptual Self-Awareness and Embodied Self-Awareness. According to Fogel,

> ***Conceptual Self-Awareness*** *is the experience of primarily thinking about our body experiences without necessarily being able to feel them.*[3] I also use the term "conceptual awareness" in this book.

> ***Embodied Self-Awareness*** *is the present-moment experiencing of sensations that arise from within our bodies, including our emotions.*[3] I also use the term "embodied awareness" in this book.

*To be **Embodied** means that experiences are felt directly as arising from within the body without intervening thought.[3]*

Many leaders easily reach conceptual self-awareness, resolutions such as "I need to slow down, I need to listen better, I need to let go of some things, I want to delegate more and empower my team, I want to be a better influencer," etc. But such conceptual awareness may not be urgent or powerful enough to drive observable positive leadership behavior change in a sustainable way.

I have consistently observed that when a leader develops embodied self-awareness, the resulting insight can be profound and life changing.

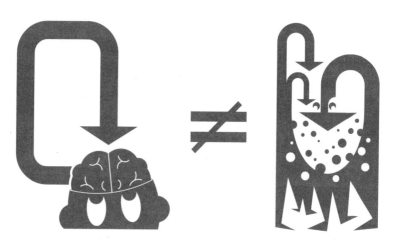

Conceptual Self-Awareness Does Not Equal Embodied Self-Awareness

DOING

DOING is how we master our relationship with the outer world, or how we play the "outer game". It is what we choose to do. This includes our chosen actions often observed in interactions with others. This is significantly influenced by how we choose to see ourselves and the world - our BEING.

While self-awareness is powerful, we often hear that "Awareness is half the battle." There remains a massive chasm between awareness and turning this awareness into real action and observable change. As effective leaders, we need to cultivate our DOING in addition to our BEING.

Research shows that about 54% of people who resolved to change their ways failed to make the transformation last beyond 6 months, and the average person made the same life resolution 10 times over without success.[4] Organizations constantly struggle with turning desired change to actual change. According to Harvard Business Review, about 70% of all organizational change initiatives fail.[5]

We may try to think our way into making changes, but this rarely works. Habits and behavior patterns are what we repeatedly do. Our habits have been wired in our brain (specifically in an area of our brain called the basal ganglia[6]) and they are ingrained and stored in our skeletal-muscular structure, our nervous system, and our entire Body over a, often, long period of time.

Building a new habit takes physical embodiment so that desired actions become embodied actions. Otherwise, we will be stuck at the level of theory, thoughts, and desires.

In my definition,

> ***Desired actions*** *are actions envisioned at a thinking or conceptual level.*

> ***Embodied actions*** *are real actions executed by the Body beyond a thinking or conceptual level. I also use the terms "physical practice" or "Embodied Leadership Practice" in this book.*

We can unleash our leadership potential and express our lives more fully by mastering the relationship between our Body and Mind in practicing Embodied Leadership. We can eliminate the significant wasted energy due to lack of congruence. We can focus on being our authentic self and leading in such a way that inspires others without having to lead "harder".

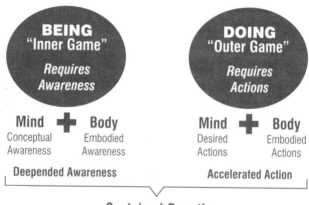

This is a book about discovering possibilities: these are stories of powerful leaders who have been able to elevate their impact and fulfillment while feeling more alive. I invite you to read this book with a beginner's Mind and a curious Body. Enjoy!

BEING

Embodied Awareness
Elevates the INNER GAME

3

INTRODUCTION TO BEING

INTRODUCTION TO BEING

BEING is the ultimate DOING.[1] *Lao Tzu*

"We are not sick because of our surface symptoms; we have symptoms because our underlying energy or Qi is imbalanced."[2] This is from an ancient Chinese medical text of the Yellow Emperor, upon which modern Chinese medicine is based.

The Indian mystic Osho compares the waves to the ocean.[3] Ocean is deep, surface waves are motion generated from friction with the environment. To me, a human being is the ocean; her emotions and actions are the surface waves.

As we interact with the outer world, we develop behavior and thinking patterns due to the frictions we encounter and emotions we experience along the way. These are like the waves on the surface of the ocean. But the ocean is so much more than the waves upon its surface.

If we go deep to the bottom of the ocean, we come to a place of stillness. This stillness is the true depth and substance of the ocean. This is our BEING space.

Deep below the surface of our conditioned behavior and thinking patterns, we discover our true nature, our essence, our best self. It has been there all along. Often, we simply forget to look and connect with it.

We can be so busy fighting the outer environment, maybe

competing with other waves to thrust higher, perhaps feeling miserable after crashing just to get ready for the next jump. The noise of engaging and fighting with the outer world numbs our ability to hear the deep quietness of the ocean, to see a much larger body of substance, to feel a much calmer presence, and to connect with a much more powerful energy. That space is the space of BEING, not DOING.

quietness of the deep ocean

Deep In the Ocean We Find a Place of Stillness

In any organization, whether large or small, for-profit or not-for-profit, leaders continuously seek to expand their leadership capacity and that of their team members. But often we go about it the wrong way. We tend to focus on the immediate issues and try to fix them without going deeper into what created them in the first place. We end up DOING more and working harder. This can be exhausting, and seldom provides a long-term solution to our challenges.

To make leadership more impactful and less taxing, we need to shift our thinking beyond DOING and look into how we are BEING, so we can have more impact without just working harder.

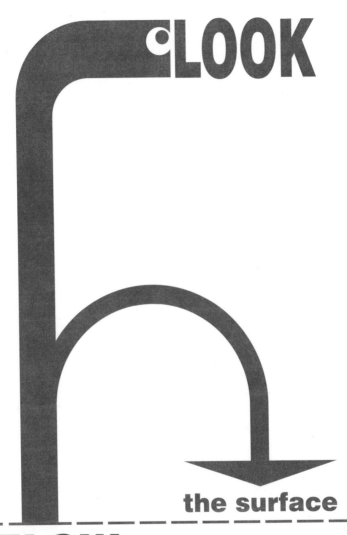

LOOK

the surface

BELOW

Great leaders are great coaches. Our work as a coaching leader is to help other leaders look below the surface and facilitate this connection between BEING and DOING, so that whatever they decide to do will come with strong conviction and will be sustainable over time.

I started to look beyond the surface waves when I was stricken with acne at the age of forty.

Story

"You Won't Treat My Acne?"

In the Chinese language, acne has an endearing term – "youth and beauty beads." This term helps make teenagers feel less self-conscious of their acne.

I had perfectly clear skin growing up, maybe due to the plentitude of moisture in the air in southern China. Then at forty, living on the opposite side of the globe – in Ohio, northern USA – I was greeted with stubborn adult acne. Was this a second youth?

After two years of struggles and trying every available commercial and medical product, thousands of dollars in treatments and many months of pills, my "youth and beauty beads" continued to be resilient.

I was introduced to Dr. Pan, a Chinese acupuncturist in her mid-fifties with radiant skin. Her warm smile made me feel comfortable right away.

She asked me a lot of questions about my lifestyle habits, physical and emotional state, temperamental tendencies, things not often asked by typical medical doctors trained in the United States. Having had exposure to Chinese medicine, I was not surprised. One pattern that surfaced in that dialogue was that whenever I did not get enough sleep, my Body would go out of balance, acne would appear and stubbornly refuse to leave. In fact, it worked overtime.

I was anxious to hear her thoughts on how it could be successfully treated.

With a gentle smile, Dr. Pan looked into my eyes and said, **"I will not treat your acne."** She paused.

"What do you mean you will not treat my acne?" I felt the disturbance within me, but I waited.

"Acne is only a symptom of your illness. It is not the root cause. We need to go underneath the surface and treat you and your system as a whole."

Dr. Pan went on to explain her treatment plan, which was to balance the Qi (or energy) along three meridian lines (energy lines) of my Body, using acupuncture.

I have never liked needles. But my desire for clear skin gave me the strength to get on the treatment table every time.

"By promoting energy flow and balancing your body," said Dr. Pan, "we treat the root cause and nurture the whole system. The acne will go away naturally, and it will benefit other parts of your body as well." She concluded with a reassuring smile.

Acne was not my enemy. It was my Body's way of telling me that something was out of balance.

Dr. Pan was serious when she gave me this important piece of advice. She said her treatment was a short-term intervention to bring my body to into balance. It was critical that I change my lifestyle (go to bed earlier) to support and sustain this balance.

I took Dr. Pan's advice to adjust my sleep schedule and to keep up with the acupuncture treatments. A couple of months later, my acne went away!

I found it intriguing to compare my efforts in attacking the superficial symptoms of acne and getting nowhere, with fundamentally improving the underlying condition that created the symptoms in the first place. It has been several years since I saw Dr. Pan, and I have been able to keep acne away!

Before we jump too quickly into the presenting issues, we need to go deeper to understand what has caused the issues to begin with. Before we address how we shift to more impactful leadership behaviors in our DOING mode (what we choose to do, "on the surface"), we must first understand and optimize our BEING (how we choose to be, "below the surface").

In Chapters 4-7, you will hear my own story and stories of other leaders who have gained powerful embodied awareness at the BEING level that changed the trajectory of their leadership and led to transformative results in leadership impact and personal fulfillment.

4

EMBODIED AWARENESS DEEPENS CONNECTION WITH *AUTHENTIC SELF*

Embodied Awareness Deepens Connection with Authentic Self

To thy own self be true.[1] *Shakespeare*

Merriam-Webster's definition of "authentic" indicates "not false or imitation" and "true to one's own personality, spirit, or character."[2] Oxford Dictionary defines authentic as "of undisputed origin".[3]

Authenticity has been explored from the ancient to the modern. The concept of authentic leadership became more widely accepted in the West since Bill George's 2003 book, *Authentic Leadership.*

According to Bill George, "Leadership is authenticity, not style." Authentic leaders have self-awareness, and they have the courage to show their emotions and vulnerability. They are mission-driven, and they focus on the long-term. They are deeply connected with their emotions and they lead with their heart, not just and their minds.[4]

I define "being authentic" as demonstrating congruence between the Mind and Body; between what we think, feel, speak, and do.

To become a more strategic thinker, we may try to schedule time for topics that are important and not urgent. This action may change behavior in the short term. However, the next

BEING AUTHENTIC IS BEING ALIGNED IN WHAT WE THINK, FEEL, SPEAK, AND DO.

YAN MASCHKE

time stress hits again, we may go right back to our behavioral comfort zone – the old habit of getting into the less important issues leaving little to no time for strategic thinking.

To elevate our influence with peers, bosses, customers, the board, or investors, we may train ourselves to use specific language and speak specific words. However, deep down, if we do not fully believe in the words we speak, our body language will come across as inauthentic to others because our language is not embodied.

The most inspiring and powerful leadership style is a style that is most authentic to us – individually. However, connecting with and sustaining that authenticity requires intentional practice.

There is more wisdom in your Body than in your deepest philosophy.[5] The Body never lies. One key to being authentic is to check and ensure congruence between the Mind and Body. When we experience embodied self-awareness, a single insight can stick with us powerfully for the rest of our lives. It is like discovering a shortcut through a park – once you see it, you cannot unsee it.

Here is a personal story of checking congruence between the Mind and Body that led to a professional transformation and allowed me to live a life beyond my dreams.

Story

My Life Formula Did Not Work!

I grew up in China and moved to the United States for graduate studies in 1995. I wanted to become a bridge between the West and the East in global business. I was twenty-two years old and spent the next twenty years proving to myself that I could survive and thrive in a foreign country. I set a goal to lead a global business for a large company by age forty – an arbitrary number I picked. Everything else was secondary, up for sacrifice.

My first work experience in the United States was during my MBA program at Michigan State University, working with Steelcase on a global logistics optimization project. At the end of the MBA program, I was offered a full-time position by four prominent companies. I accepted the offer from management consultancy A.T. Kearney (now Kearney). I remember my jaw dropping when hearing the compensation offer on the phone from a Kearney partner. I was glad that she could not see my face, and my pause hopefully came across as poise. When the MBA Placement Office told me that I received the highest salary offer in my graduating class, I said quietly to myself, "Now, I really need to prove myself!"

I loved the intellectual horsepower at Kearney, working with Fortune 200 companies. I learned quickly how to solve problems regardless of industry. I learned to lead clients from the "front", "behind", and the "side," all the while making them feel they are leading. I also learned to squeeze in laundry time between conference calls on the weekends.

I left consulting after two years and joined Eaton Corporation – as my goal was to be a bridge between the West and the East for a major multinational firm in global business. Eaton is a diversified industrial corporation with $20+ billion in revenue. I followed guidance from great mentors and rounded out functional skills in global supply chain, global marketing, operations and greenfield start-up, post-acquisition integration, strategic planning, and global product line management.

During the twelve years with Eaton, I loved the accomplishments, the learning, the culture, and great mentors. I was commuting most of the time, coming home on the weekends. When my daughter was born, the commute became incredibly challenging emotionally and physically, despite the intellectual satisfaction.

I was pursued by an executive search firm to join another global manufacturing firm Nordson ($2 billion in revenue). It was an ideal job title to manage a global business with no need to commute. I was just turning forty - the random number I had chosen to reach my dream job. It felt like the stars were aligned. I made the transition.

After I started my dream job for a while, I was lost. I looked around me with a strong sense of emptiness. I did not know what was next, I had lost my light. All my life, the formula in my Mind was "work super hard, become successful, and find fulfillment." To achieve a sense of fulfillment was a dream, though I never knew what it would look or feel like. The formula did not work. It felt like the rug had been pulled out from underneath me. I was wholly disoriented.

THE FORMULA DID NOT WORK!

work super hard   become successful   find fulfillment

Two of the three years at my last corporate position involved soul-searching, intertwined with a period of depression. No one besides my husband could see this since I was high-functioning and knew how to put on a smiley face.

I was doing the right things as a business leader, but I did not feel fulfilled and I did not feel I was making the impact I desired. On the surface, I was being a bridge between the West and the East in global business; but deep inside I did not feel the integration within myself — I was too focused on DOING and forgot about BEING. I ignored the fact that I did not have congruence between my Mind and Body.

My Mind was satisfied with the achievement and the job title, but deeper within me, my heart was longing for something else - something greater. My Body was giving me warning signs in various ways that I failed to interpret. I experienced bouts of crying, Body pain, and a lack of energy. It was not until I hit my rock bottom that I came to a physical realization that this could not continue, and I needed to shake it off and get myself re-aligned.

On that journey of soul searching, I continuously felt the pain of not making the impact or achieving the fulfillment I desired. The pain was real, it was felt in my Body.

It was not until I re-examined my core values, drives, and my gifts that I could re-establish my purpose and vision, based on a deep understanding of who I am and what I am here for.

It was not until I experienced that tremendous pain physically and emotionally that I was able to answer a powerful question, "What is the pain in the world that you want to help alleviate?" The answer came through my Body, "The pain in the world I want to help alleviate is the pain I am having right now! Successful leaders yearning for greater impact and fulfillment."

Vision	Life fully expressed. A world more connected.
Purpose	To help leaders unlock their potential.
Values	Authenticity, Presence, Connectedness.
Drives	Creativity, Expression, Accomplishments.
Gifts	Bringing out the best in leaders and teams.
Pain	Successful leaders yearning for greater impact and fulfillment.

In that pain, I wished I had a coach; I wished my boss had a coach, and I wished our executive team had a coach. So, I became one.

I committed to a mission to help other senior leaders and leadership teams achieve greater impact. I knew I could do this as an executive coach, leadership team coach, and a strategy facilitator. I experienced a transformation in how I show up every day, and how I see and interact with the world. I shifted from a goal-driven machine to a purpose-driven human.

My emotional and physical pain informed and guided me towards a clear sense of inner compass and calling – a sense of direct knowing beyond rational thinking that is viscerally and undeniably real. It had evolved from a conceptual awareness of being a bridge between the West and the East to an embodied awareness of helping leaders fully express their lives in a holistic and authentic way.

The subconscious question I woke up to every day for so many years was "How can I get to that job title faster?" Now, the conscious question I ask myself every day is "How can I make my highest contribution in the time I have left?"

I am no longer seeking fulfillment. Instead, I live it every day. It was not until after I connected with the sense of calling in an embodied way that I realized that bringing out the best in people and teams has always been my gift. My twenty plus years of corporate and consulting experience was the perfect training for what I am called to do. My life in both the East and West has forged a unique ability to hold different perspectives and help others expand theirs. A lifelong pursuit of wholeness and various forms of Mind-Body practices has trained me to be highly attuned to my own energy and that of others, which allows a unique possibility to help others accelerate transformational results at both an individual and systemic level.

Instead of having an impact leading one business, I am now able to impact many businesses globally by supporting many powerful clients through advisory, coaching, and facilitation. It is a humbling privilege to be able to help other leaders breathe life into their leadership. As coaching leaders, we all have that honor and responsibility. It is sacred work.

Leadership Lesson
Authenticity = Congruence

In our congruent "BEING", "Mind" represents our thoughts, beliefs, perspectives, and mindset; "Body" represents the associated feelings and physical sensations, how we are aware of them and work with them. When there is congruence between the Body and Mind, we live and lead authentically.

After feeling the pain of not achieving the desired impact and fulfillment, I was able to connect with a sense of congruence between my Mind and Body and feel completely aligned. My father-in-law perceptively observed that I was no longer talking about when I could save enough money to retire, because I would want to do what I do for as long as I live. My husband and daughter both told me that I am working more than ever, I was surprised because I do not feel that I am working at all. I am simply doing meaningful work, expressing life authentically, and feeling incredibly alive.

The Body doesn't lie. Check in with your Body to see if your words, actions, feelings, and thoughts are aligned. Go below the surface to understand where any misalignment resides and explore possibilities of congruence.

BEING is how we choose to be. When we are congruence between the Mind and Body, we are more grounded and confident. Our commitment to action has power and life behind it, and we show up as our most authentic and powerful self.

Embodied Leadership Practice
Mind-Body Aligned Decisions

1. Pick a decision you need to make. A decision can be as simple as what to say when preparing for an important discussion.

2. Invite a partner to support you.

   a. Your partner can take notes for you as you speak and can share any observations about you as you speak – such as your body language, tone, and energy.

3. Name and label your final two options in your decision.

4. Pick an option and answer each of the 3 questions below. You can use Table 1 to capture notes.

   a. As you think of this option, what emerges in your Mind? This is about your thinking, maybe the pros and cons of the option at a rational level.

   b. As you think of this option, what emerges in your Body? What feelings and physical sensations do you notice in your Body? This includes both external and internal sensations, including in the areas of your heart, gut, and your whole Body.

   c. Notice any alignment or conflict between the insights from the Mind and the Body as you explore.

5. Go to the second option and answer questions above.

6. Pause, take a deep breath. Discuss with your partner about any insights you have gained from this exercise as you explored the options. Invite your partner to share any observations they have. Use these insights to help you make your decision.

Table 1

	OPTION 1	OPTION 2
MIND		
BODY		
INSIGHTS	

5

EMBODIED AWARENESS BOOSTS

EMOTIONAL INTELLIGENCE

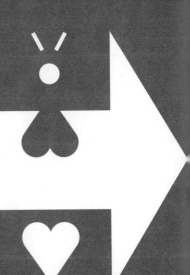

Embodied Awareness Boosts
Emotional Intelligence

Whoever lets herself be led by the heart will never lose her way.[1] Egyptian Proverb

Author Daniel Goleman has written persuasively about the connection between emotional intelligence and leadership. Emotional intelligence is twice as important as technical skills or IQ for jobs at all levels. At top tiers, it accounts for nearly 90% of the difference between average and star performers.[2] Companies who have executives with higher levels of emotional intelligence are more likely to be highly profitable.[3]

To develop our emotional intelligence, we need to become self-aware of our emotions; cultivate self-regulation emotionally and behaviorally; practice empathy towards others; and build social skills. So, step one is becoming self-aware of our emotions.

Emotions are felt within the Body and often have associated physical sensations. According to noted neurologist Antonio Damasio, emotional reactions are "automatic and unconscious" and our recognition of a feeling "can emerge only after the brain registers physical changes in the body."[4]

We can better develop our emotional intelligence through tapping into the powerful intelligence of our Body.

Emotional intelligence requires emotional self-awareness. Emotional self-awareness requires emotional literacy – ability to name your emotions. Emotional literacy is enhanced by our ability to be attuned to our physical sensations because emotions always have accompanying neurophysiological sensations. In other words, Embodied Self-Awareness, as defined in Chapter 2, brings life into Conceptual Self-Awareness, and puts fire behind it.

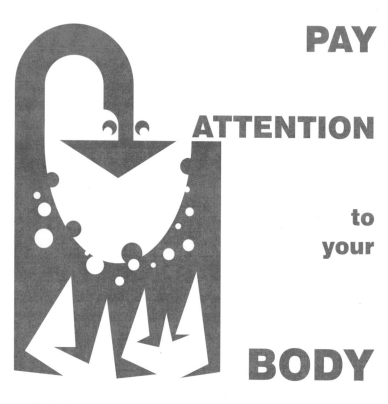

PAY
ATTENTION
to
your
BODY

In the following story, you will see how getting in touch with emotions in an embodied way accelerated a leader's self-awareness and enhanced his leadership effectiveness.

Story
"How Else Can I Provide?"

Michael is a key engineering leader for an award-winning technology infrastructure company. In his late thirties, with a medium build, and a deep and resounding voice that can be heard halfway down the hall. His beard covers at least the lower half of his face but is unable to mask his genuine broad smiles.

The CEO of the company sees Michael as a critical leader to the growth of the company and hired me to work with Michael to accelerate his development. Michael would like to elevate his emotional intelligence and lead through more effective delegation.

Michael and I met in his office for our introductory meeting. I had prepared some typical topics for discussion: confidentiality, coaching process and approach, logistics, and his desired outcomes.

He welcomed me in, with a bright voice and contagious smile. My eyes were immediately drawn to a large size family photo in a beautiful glass frame on the wall behind him. There he was with his beautiful wife and their adorable young children. Michael was very proud to speak about his family.

We sat down at the round table in his office, next to his computer workstation.

Michael expressed his lack of familiarity with coaching and confusion between coaching and consulting. We briefly discussed this and he came to understand that coaching is a facilitated learning process, to help bring out the best of what is already within him, not a teaching process to fix him or to tell him what to do.

From that point on, Michael's energy started to guide our conversation. We did not get to any of the other topics I had prepared. Michael started to say that one of the reflective questions I emailed him (I typically send some questions before the first meeting to get the client's thinking started) really got him thinking.

The question was: "What do you care about that's keeping you up at night?" He handed me a copy of his answers and started talking.

"What keeps me up at night is providing for my family."

His parents had emigrated from Eastern Europe. After coming to the United States, his father opened and operated a convenience store, and Michael worked in the store from ages ten to twenty in addition to keeping up with his studies. He did not engage in any leisure activities or have much time with friends. He grew up working hard. Discipline and responsibility were two of the highest virtues engrained in him.

Michael felt deeply grateful to his wife and their children. He turned his head toward the big family photo on the wall, then turned back, trying to hold back his tears.

"I would do anything for my family." He paused for the first time in our conversation. His Body was quiet, his gaze still, his face filled with deep conviction. There was a palpable sense of sacredness in the air. We honored it with pure silence.

Michael was one of the earliest employees of the company. It was clear that he cared deeply about what he does and the people with whom he works. He worked super hard over the years to support the company's growth, and to "provide" for his family.

Michael was managing five direct reports and sometimes found himself doing their jobs. He wanted to help them succeed and help other leaders in the company succeed, as his colleagues were like family to him. The congruence between his body language and his words reflected his genuineness. He said he wanted to step into the next level of leadership, and that he needed to reduce his workload.

I was fully present, without saying a word. I listened with my heart and I let myself experience his emotions within my own Body.

Michael's energy informed me that he was ready to take a little break from talking. I first acknowledged his authenticity and courage to share his story, and I told him that I was deeply moved.

I asked if it was OK for me to share an observation. Michael said "Yes". I shared that I understood how important it was for him to "provide" for his family, and that I was picking up a sense that the word "provide" for him primarily referenced providing financial support for his family. I checked in with him to see how my observation landed.

Michael paused. Looking at me with his head slightly tilted, he agreed this was true now that I had pointed it out and he had thought about it.

"Where do you think you are in your ability to provide financially for your family?" I asked.

This time Michael was speaking a bit more slowly, almost speaking and reflecting at the same time.

"I think I have done a great job providing financially for my family. I know I am at a great place to be able to continue to provide for my family.

"Somehow subconsciously I was still carrying that old sense of insecurity, the sense that I need to work super hard in order to be OK. Subconsciously, I even worry whether I would lose my job if I didn't work this hard."

I followed with a gentle question. "What do you think, rationally, is the possibility of you losing your job?"

"Very small," Michael said confidently. "I am a critical part of the company. Not only will I not lose my job, but I also think the company would appreciate me more if I learned to let go of some work and step up more strategically as a senior leader."

Michael had the look of an "Aha" moment.

I asked, "If you were to put yourself back into the shoes of the ten-year-old you, working in your Dad's convenience store, in what ways do you wish he could have provided for YOU besides financially?"

I could hear the running of his computer station, and I could feel the turning up of emotions inside of Michael. I felt them in my Body - my chest, my head, and my eyes.

Michael's presence said it all. The energetic field around us was imbued with his emotions.

Finally, he said, "I know what you mean. All these years, I was only thinking of providing in a financial way, in order to give a sense of safety. The reality is that I have already done that, I have done that very well. I can provide in other ways."

I honored his presence with mine. "In what ways do you think you can provide to your children beyond financial security?"

Michael started to share how he enjoyed teaching his older daughter Sierra to ride a bicycle. It brought him tremendous fulfillment and he knew it was meaningful for Sierra.

I followed his energy. "What was that moment like, when you finally decided to let go of holding Sierra on the bike and let her ride on her own?"

"It was scary. I was afraid she would fall and get hurt."

"How did you know that it was OK and it was time to let go when you were afraid of her being hurt?" I asked.

Michael gave this a bit of thought. "I wasn't far away, if she fell, I could quickly get to her. At some point, I had to let her go on her own for her to grow." His words sounded sure.

I asked, "I wonder how that might relate to your leadership with your direct reports at the company?"

A silence full of insight. "Yeah." A deep sigh. Michael turned his head slightly down, as if to directly examine his reflections.

"I tend to jump in too quickly to help, to do the work, to solve the problem. Subconsciously I may be trying to protect them too much. It's been a habit from so many years of jumping in and getting things done that I am not even conscious of it anymore." Michael's Body was relaxed, his gaze softened. His family photo on the wall behind him smiled at us gently.

"I need to let go of that subconscious need to protect, to secure the outcome, to 'provide' the outcome for the company."

I felt compelled to acknowledge that I was privileged to witness this moment. This whole conversation felt sacred. I spoke slowly and deliberately.

"I can see that you have a big heart. You care deeply about the people around you. In the past, you may not have let people see the soft side of you. But that does not change the fact you have the capacity to experience deep emotions, your genuine desire to connect with people at the heart-to-heart level. You can be powerful in your DOING - what you choose to do, and you can also be powerful in your BEING - how you choose to be."

Michael looked up. His office seemed to have brightened suddenly, as if a ray of sunshine brushed through the space.

I could tell that he deeply appreciated my acknowledgement. He seemed surprised by what he was learning about himself. I honored that sacred space by holding my presence and extending that moment of silence between us.

Moments later, I took my question a bit further, "In what ways might you be willing to provide for your colleagues, not just in helping them get things done, but also in providing in emotional ways?"

Michael sat up a bit taller and smiled. He was energized.

At the end of the meeting, it felt like months had passed – it was almost surreal.

Michael decided he would spend more quality time with his family the following weekend. He also made a commitment to himself to provide for his team in different ways than before, by providing emotional support through listening and showing compassion, by doing less and delegating more.

When asked about his main learning from our conversation, Michael paused, then spoke excitedly.

"I always looked at 'providing' in financial terms. Now I can look at providing in emotional terms – both with my family and my work family. I have climbed up the hill of providing financially. Now the next hill to climb is to provide emotionally."

I always looked at "providing" in financial terms. Now I can look at providing in emotional terms.

Before I left his office, I asked Michael how his first coaching experience compared with his expectation. He said he thought it would be more like a lecture, and this was not.

"Actually," he said. "I have never had a conversation like this with anyone in my life. It opened my eyes. It's life changing."

It opened my eyes. It's life changing.

At the end of our coaching program, Michael received great feedback from his stakeholders with whom he engaged throughout the six months we worked together. 100% of Michael's stakeholders have said that he has elevated leadership effectiveness in each of the areas he focused on. Other leaders now come to Michael for guidance and coaching. A few months after our engagement completed, Michael called me excitedly. He had received a promotion that day and wanted to make sure to tell me right away!

As an interesting side note, I met Michael's wife at a company party, and she shared that her husband became a different person at home (in a very good way) since he started coaching with me.

LEADERSHIP LESSON
Lead with Embodied Emotional Intelligence

There is a quote that has been attributed to many people including President Theodore Roosevelt, "No one cares how much you know, until they know how much you care."[5]

To inspire others and to lead powerfully, we need to engage our team members emotionally. To do that, we need to be able to connect with our own emotions; engage others from that space, and embody what we think and feel in what we do and speak.

Great leaders are great coaches. We have the responsibility and privilege to help others expand their leadership capacity, invite them to see different perspectives, and facilitate their self-discovery. We can help leaders connect with their own emotions and with what they deeply care about in an embodied way. There, they can access their higher power within. As Frederic Laloux said, "As human beings, we are not problems waiting to be solved, but potential waiting to unfold."[6]

In our conversation, Michael could have stayed on the level of the Mind and brainstormed actions for the challenges at hand. Instead, he accessed his power at a deeper level through exploring his emotional experiences with his father and daughter, in a way that was deeply felt in his Body.

Something in his BEING was driving Michael's shift in

perspective. Everything he needed was already inside of him. He just didn't know how he could access it. During our coaching conversation, his emotional experience became felt and embodied. This helped him uncover what was inside, the emotions and feelings he carried in his Body.

As human beings, we are not problems waiting to be solved, but potential waiting to unfold. *Frederic Laloux*

Emotions are often felt in the Body.[7] Accessing a strong emotion in a fully embodied way can deepen our awareness and create an opening for a powerful shift in our perspectives.

Michael felt his emotions in a way he never had before, in his entire Body, nervous sytem – his whole BEING. In our first coaching conversation, I witnessed massive stillness and a new opening within Michael. He shifted into a different realm of consciousness, in an immediate, present, embodied, and undeniable way. That deep insight and embodied awareness outside of the professional context was then able to be applied to the challenges he faced at work.

As embodied self-awareness goes deep into our BEING, the resulting commitment to action has tremendous power and life behind it. Ultimately, it makes DOING much easier and far more sustainable.

Shifting to Your Embodied Consciousness

For Michael, the embodied self-awareness was followed by amazing positive behavior change, oberved by his colleagues with overwhelming validation. In his final coaching assessment, he reported:

"Our sessions expanded my horizon and opened my peripheral vision. Instead of just straight ahead, I can now look sideways and up, and I have developed more strategic thinking. I can better lead my team through delegation, communication, and trust. My outlook has become positive and I am motivated."

Embodied self-awareness helped Michael choose a new way of BEING. Our integrative Mind-Body intelligence helps us see and feel more fully and helps us engage and lead with our heart.

Embodied Leadership Practice
Get in Touch with Your Feelings

1. Who has made a meaningful impact on your life and how has this person had an impact on you?

    a. Specifically, how did this person make you feel and how did that feeling impact you? You can write down notes on a piece of paper.

2. How would you like to make others feel if you were to engage and lead someone (or a team) at work? How would that affect this person's work and ability to achieve results? How might that affect him/her as a person beyond work?

3. If the above impact is energizing for you, what does it mean to you in action? What is one small step you can take to move in that direction?

    a. How confident are you that you will take that small step?

    b. How will you hold yourself accountable to that small action?

The goal of this exercise is to connect with something that has touched you emotionally in a way that may enable you to rise from that insight and engage with others at a heart-to-heart level.

Note: You can also facilitate this discussion with your team as a whole. You can start with introducing your intent for this exercise. Then, you can split them into pairs using the questions above to guide their discussions. The pairs can switch roles between the person asking the questions and the person answering the questions. Finally, bring the pairs back to the larger group to share their insights from discussions.

6

**EMBODIED
AWARENESS
ENHANCES**

*EXECUTIVE
PRESENCE*

Embodied Awareness Enhances
Executive Presence

If you are calm and rooted, you can lead in any situation.[1] *Lao Tzu*

It was said that former United States President Abraham Lincoln interviewed someone for a cabinet position in 1860. He did not hire that person because he did not like how that candidate put himself together. He said, "I don't like his face." When his advisors argued "The poor man isn't responsible for his face," Lincoln said that "Every man over 40 is responsible for his face."[2]

There are many definitions of "executive presence". Leaders may refer to different scope when they use the phrase "executive presence", sometimes they may use that as a "catch all" phrase for general soft skills.

Former CEO of GE, Jack Welch calls executive presence one of the top two things needed to advance your career. He declares, "It is a fingerprint of you".[3]

Known for her 2012 TedTalk *"Your Body Language May Shape Who You Are"* and her book *"Presence"*, Harvard social psychologist Amy Cuddy defines presence as "the state of being attuned to and able to comfortably express our true thoughts, feelings, values and potential."[4] Cuddy does not see a difference between "executive presence" and "presence". She states that presence happens when our nonverbal and verbal behaviors become synchronized; she believes that presence can be enhanced by simply tweaking our body language, behavior, and mindset in our day-to-day lives.[5]

In the context of our discussion in this book, executive presence is how we hold ourselves and the energy field we project around us, that inevitably influences others and impacts our collective ability to reach meaningful common goals.

Executive presence is how we hold ourselves and the energy field we project around us, that inevitably influences others and impacts our collective ability to reach meaningful common goals.

Yan Maschke

In the framework of "Interpersonal Neurobiology", there is a flow of energy and information formed through neurocircuitry as we interact with others. That flow is then shared and regulated between people through engagement, connection, and communication.[6] "Emotional Contagion" is the phenomenon of having one person's emotions and related behaviors directly trigger similar emotions and behaviors in other people.[7] In ancient Chinese wisdom, we are energy beings. We carry an energetic presence, and we project an energy field that influences others around us.

All the actions we take and all the words we speak are executed by the Body. Cultivating our presence requires attunement to ourselves and fluency in the language of the Body. When we are centered and congruent between the Mind and the Body, we can access our best self and exude our most authentic presence. However, since majority of our behavior is the result of habits, instincts, and other unconscious patterns,[8] most of us are not often consciously choosing how we are showing up from moment to moment.

Our Body stores these habits, instincts, and behavior patterns. A behavior pattern is developed over time, often as a conditioned response to the circumstances and the world around us. It shows up as an impulse or urge. It is part of our survival and coping strategy. The cognitive brain is too limited because such urges often show up before we have had a chance to recruit our full cognitive faculties. When we are trying to change a conditioned behavior, we are often working with habits or urges that are 10, 30, or even 50 years old.

Authentic presence requires moment-to-moment awareness of what is happening within us, so we can swiftly shift ourselves from our conditioned tendencies to our desired state of presence.

Good intentions are not enough. We need to change the habits where the habits are stored – the Body. To make meaningful lasting change – such as cultivating authentically powerful executive presence – we need to gain deep self-awareness to access a powerful shift and real change. This story below is an example of cultivating both embodied awareness and embodied actions to enhance executive presence.

Story

"I Am Very Nervous at Board Meetings"

Amber is a high-performing supply chain management executive for a medium-sized industrial manufacturing firm. Young but mature, well-dressed, and professional. She had recently been promoted and joined the executive team. She had developed a great reputation with the CEO and her colleagues. Amber was known for her ability to accomplish a tremendous amount while displaying strong emotional and social intelligence – not an easy combination.

With her promotion, Amber needed to interact with the board quite often, but she found one board member particularly intimidating - a member from the parent private equity firm. According to her CEO, she often became nervous before board meetings and was visibly nervous during the board meetings. After the board meetings, she would then feel bad and "beat herself up" over the fact that she was nervous, which seemed to add to her stress and did not help the situation.

I had the pleasure of working with Amber to help her enhance executive presence.

Amber and I embarked on a learning journey. We explored her mindset and her emotions. What I learned about her is that presence is a strength of hers in general. She presents herself very well; she is confident, professional, calm, and collected. Her challenge lies in applying her natural strength of presence in unfamiliar high-stake situations - such as when interacting with the board and sometimes with senior executives at customer organizations.

Her brain seems to perceive and anticipate whatever questions may come from that board member as a potential attack, an invisible wall goes up in front of her, her Body tightens and gets triggered into its automatic reaction of self-defense. In that moment, she freezes and is not her normal resourceful, creative, and powerful self. By the way, have you ever experienced this? Most of us have at one time or another.

We first explored this at a rational or Mind level. It was hard for her to translate that level of insight into real action in-the-moment. She knew what she wanted and needed to do – her desired actions were clear, but she just could not get her Body to do it. An automatic reaction seemed always to take over.

At one point during our coaching engagement, I asked if she was open to an Experiential Coaching session, which is a facilitated coaching session where the client experiences deepened self-awareness through the present-moment body sensations, often in a venue outside of typical work environment. All she needed to do was to pick a venue based on her personal interest, and we would have some fun.

Amber told me that she found inspiration from yoga. So, we decided to have a yoga Experiential Coaching session. Amber arranged for us to attend a group yoga class at a studio that she frequented.

I knew we could not talk during the group class, so I sat down with Amber briefly before the class started.

Since her brain seemed to react to the "unknown questions" from the board member as if reacting to a physical attack, we discussed the principles of energy management, the power of grounding energy, and how martial artists learn to dissipate incoming or attacking energy downward through the ground. We doodled on paper.

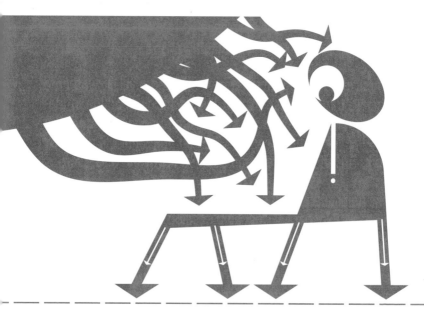

Managing the Energies of Your Body Through the Ground

Then I asked if there was a yoga pose that was challenging to her. She said the Pigeon pose presented her with the greatest difficulty in her practice. I asked what she does when she is in that challenging pose. She said she would "fight through it".

Language is powerful. If her internal language is to "fight

through it", her Body's reaction is naturally to "fight".

We explored how we could shift her energy to help her with the challenging pose. She decided that she would try to "embrace" the challenging energy and then diffuse that energy to the ground through her Body.

"Let's see what happens!" Off we went to the class.

Wow, I learned that Amber is good at yoga!

Clearly, I was the one who struggled more with poses than Amber did. Amber even whispered to me to help me with a couple of my poses.

Rolling up our mats, wiping of some well-earned sweat, Amber and I sat down to debrief after the class ended.

I asked Amber what her experience was especially with the pigeon pose.

Amber said she tried to shift her energy in the challenging position. She was able to play with embracing and grounding the challenging energy. She found it easier to get into and stay in the pigeon pose, and she became calmer and felt more confident as a result.

LEARN TO SHIFT YOUR ENERGY

Leadership Lesson
Stillness Welcomes All things

Executive presence is often viewed as the secret power of leadership. It has multiple dimensions, with the most visible part being how we hold ourselves as leaders, and how we project an energetic field around us to influence and inspire others.

Executive presence is an energy. Our Body is the temple for our soul and our energy. Our presence is carried by our Body in a physical and energetic way. As a result, a powerful way to enhance our executive presence is to access it through our Body. When we can be completely in the moment and fully access that energy of stillness and rootedness, we can be most flexible and resourceful, we can welcome all things and lead in any situation. This energy can be sensed and read by those around us. Sometimes this is called charisma.

Amber's embodied awareness from our yoga Experiential Coaching session was: Do not fight. Let yourself breathe, channel the fighting energy down to the ground, and welcome new choices and possibilities.

Moving forward, we explored how Amber could take her embodied learning and practice from the mat to the board room – mentally, emotionally, physically, and energetically.

Now, before a board meeting, Amber breathes intentionally and lets the anxiety go through her Body to the ground. When a challenging question comes, she remembers her embodied awareness from our yoga experience. The first step is to notice the "fighting" urge through her Body – physical sensations that accompany that urge and her automatic behavior pattern. She starts to breathe intentionally to ground her energy. Taking grounding breaths was her embodied action and served as a bridge between the yoga mat and board room. By taking a few deep breaths, she could remind herself of the feeling and sensations of "embracing" and "grounding" on the yoga mat and bring that online through her Body while being challenged with a question in the board room.

Once she is able to shift her energy through the embodied action of intentionally breathing and grounding, many possibilities start to open up and she can make a conscious choice of her narratives and actions. She can then choose to detach from her nervousness and focus on listening to the board member's question. She can acknowledge the question and ask a clarifying question to better understand the intent behind the question vs. jumping immediately into a defensive mode. She is able to act from her most resourceful and powerful self because she is centered at a BEING level, and she can embody her desired presence.

As you read this, you may say, "But I don't do yoga!" No problem. You do not need to do yoga. We can all breathe and access the grounding energy in anything we do – sports, exercise, cooking, gardening, reading, sitting, standing, walking, talking, you name it. We all have a Body, don't we?

Breathe deeply. Feel the weight of gravity on your Body. Allow your breath to bring your energy to the ground. You can use any form of physical or energetic practice that you like. In recent years, we have been hearing the term "mindfulness practice" in the West. If you take a closer look, all mindfulness practices are about getting into your Body in the present moment!

Your Body is your friend. You do not need to look far and beyond. Your true power is right within you, and you can access it right here, right now!

Embodied Leadership Practice
Grounded Presence

1. Think of a person or an upcoming situation that makes you a bit nervous.

2. Imagine you are meeting with that person or in that upcoming situation. Allow yourself to be nervous. Take inventory of what you feel and sense inside your Body. Name and acknowledge those sensations. Be specific.

   a. It is easy to name a feeling (such as "I am nervous"), it takes some intentionality to name the actual sensations that accompany that feeling. Do you have a sweaty palm? Does your heartbeat hasten? What happens to your breathing? What shifts in your posture? What is happening with the volume, pitch, pace, and quality of your voice? Where is your eye gaze? How tight or loose are your facial muscles and those on your shoulders and back?

   b. No self-criticism, only self-compassion. Acknowledge and honor the state you are in right now.

   c. Emotional intelligence requires emotional self-awareness. Emotional self-awareness requires emotional literacy – ability to name your emotions. Emotional literacy is enhanced by embodied awareness because emotions always have accompanying neurophysiological sensations.

3. Take a few deep breaths. Close your eyes. Feel the grounding energy in your Body. Notice your slower breathing and more relaxed Body. Continue for a minute or two.

4. Open your eyes and notice your state of being physically grounded.

5. Now imagine you are in the situation described in step 2 above. How is your presence different from before? What did you do that led to this shift?

6. Practice this repeatedly before you need to step into the upcoming real-life situation.

In real-life situations, before you go into the actual meeting or situation, allow yourself a few minutes and practice Steps 3-4 above. Bring your grounded presence.

There are four ways to use this practice:

1. You can use this exercise for yourself.

2. You can share this exercise with others.

3. You can facilitate this exercise with someone else.

4. You can facilitate this exercise in a group by dividing people into practice pairs.

7

EMBODIED AWARENESS
SUPPORTS
LEADING CHANGE

Embodied Awareness Supports
Leading Change

Change is the only constant in life.[1] *Heraclitus*

Leadership is about leading change.

Being aware of our own feelings and those of others is a critical part of developing emotional intelligence and it is highly relevant in leading change.

About 70% of all organizational change initiatives fail.[2] According to Harvard Business Review, this has been a consistent statistic since the 1970's. "The content of change management is reasonably correct, but the managerial capacity to implement it has been woefully underdeveloped."[3]

Organizational change requires skillful change agents and success critically relies on change agents' ability to facilitate individual behavior change. People do not like change done to them. Change brings fear.

As change leaders, it is critical for us to understand the biggest resistance to change – fear. We not only need to be aware of how fear shows up in ourselves as we lead change, but also how fear can show up in the people we lead, so we can help them manage and take action despite fear.

Fear is experienced in our Body. Some of our most powerful

physical sensations are those associated with fear. When we are scared, we shiver and sweat, and our hearts pump hard. Our brain interprets these sensations. Such physical sensations can lead to a "fight, flight or, freeze" response and trigger a narrative such as "I am scared, I can't do this." Feelings, sensations, and thoughts are integrated, not isolated.

Much like stress, fear is embodied - in an instinctual and automatic way that precedes our rational decision making (often we are not consciously choosing to be fearful). According to author A.J. Jacobs, when working with such automatic reactions and habitual patterns, "It is easier to act your way into a new thinking than to think your way into a new action."[4]

To learn how to cope with our fear and to take action despite fear, we first need to gain embodied self-awareness of how fear shows up and its impact. Then we have a choice to access new possibilities.

Embodied Awareness of Fear

Story

"There Is No Way I Can Dance!"

I had the privilege to work with the senior leadership team of a prestigious hospitality organization for two years.

During a half-day leadership team coaching and facilitation session, we had about 45 minutes left. I invited the team to "play" a little and do some experiential learning through dancing, I would show them a few dance moves and they would try to learn, and we would debrief along the way any leadership lessons we learned. I made sure there was a large open space in the conference room so we could move around and spread out.

Most of the people stood up from their chairs and started to walk towards the open space in the center of the room.

One leader, Cadence, was clearly hesitant. She stood up but was walking very slowly. "Well, there is... no way... that I am gonna be able to... dance..." A sense of frozenness in her voice. Even the classical oil painting portraits on the wall seemed to be leaning in to observe.

Others were quiet, waiting to hear my response.

Without frustration or attachment, I said, "It is up to us whether we want to play. It's really not about learning how to dance, it's about the leadership lessons we might learn while we try to learn to dance." My voice was calm, low, and slow.

"As you consider this, just notice what's happening with you, and what's emerging inside of you." I added.

"I know dancing is something unfamiliar to many of us and it feels outside of our control. It is a change from our routine. Just notice how we are showing up and what's happening within us." I continued the encouragement.

The team members continued to walk towards the center silently, forming two lines as I had suggested. So did Cadence.

I held the shared space for a few moments of silence.

The voice of the general manager broke the silence, "My heart is racing. I am really nervous." His voice was low but cut through the air like a laser beam.

I acknowledged the general manager for his vulnerability and courage to share his feelings and sensations. As his words resonated among the others, there was a sense of aliveness with everyone underneath the quietness in the room.

"Notice how we naturally react to something unfamiliar or a change. Now imagine people two or three levels down below us. When we roll out changes that are completely new and unfamiliar to them, let's imagine how they will feel and react," I paused slightly, "and what we can do as senior leaders to make the process of change easier for them to embrace."

The team was silent, standing in two lines. I could feel their quiet breathing and sense their neurophysiological aliveness, as an electric current in the room.

We had not even started learning any dance moves yet, we dove right into live-action coaching in the moment. Even now, as I write about this story, I can still feel the energy with the team in the room on that late morning.

We did learn a few dance moves together. The leaders rotated between being a leader and a follower, and they drew various leadership lessons from their dance learning experience. There are so many relevant and powerful leadership lessons from dancing, such as leading with your core, giving direction not force, staying in tune with your partner(s), the art of following as a leader, not forgetting the music, etc., I am planning to write a separate book about that in the future.

Later, the team said the most impactful part of that day was the experiential learning involving dancing.

By directly experiencing something in the Body, leaders can feel more alive and gain far more powerful insight, rather than just being a talking head in the conference room.

Leadership Lesson
Understand Resistance

Our observable behaviors are how we interact with the outside world and how others experience us. They are like the waves on the surface of the ocean. Underneath this surface, the ocean runs deep. Therein lie our thoughts, beliefs, perspectives, and mindsets, as well as the seat of our fears. These currents are subconscious and can control us like an invisible hand, in ways that both serve and hinder us. Carl G. Jung once said that "Until you make the unconscious conscious, it will direct your life and you will call it fate."[5]

Until you make the unconscious conscious, it will direct your life and you will call it fate.

Carl Jung

The magic is in examining the subconscious and making a choice for what will best serve us. This is the place where transformation happens, this is where we face our fear and take action despite it.

In a direct, immersive, and embodied experience, in this case, dancing, the leaders showed up as their whole selves. Their subconscious thinking, feeling, and behavior patterns came along with them. An experienced coach can facilitate learning and call out the subconscious for the leaders to examine.

Experience Yourself in an Embodied Way

When we have an opportunity to fully experience ourselves in an embodied way, we can reflect on how we have chosen to be, gain powerful embodied awareness of our own emotions and resistance, which also helps us gain awareness on how others may experience emotions and resistance as we lead them through change.

When we can understand the experiences of those impacted by the change, we can help them work through what is in the way. Change becomes easier for them to embrace, and we do not need to push as hard.

A simple Embodied Leadership Practice is to put yourself in the Body of others – those who will be impacted by the change, to feel their resistance in an embodied way, including their sensations, feelings, and thinking.

Embodied Leadership Practice
Put on Their Body

1. Is there a change initiative that you are leading for which you want to ensure buy-in and success?

2. List the key stakeholders or stakeholder groups for this change effort (people who will be affected and/or need to be involved) and draw them on a piece of paper based on the dynamics in the organization.

    a. Do not make it complicated. If all the stakeholders are at a similar level, you can draw them as if they are sitting at a conference table. If most are in the same group and a couple are outside of the group, show it that way visually on paper. If there are multiple levels of people being impacted or involved, you can use layers as in an organizational chart.

3. Embody the role of someone in a stakeholder group, such as someone from whom you have concerns about getting buy-in. Put on her Body. Walk like her, sit and stand like her, talk like her, think like her, feel like her.

4. Imagine this person's reaction to this change initiative that you are leading.

    a. You are sitting in her position and standing in her shoes.

    b. Notice any points of resistance from her perspective.

c. Write down what you experience as this person – her thinking, feeling, and her physical sensations.

d. Imagine how she might respond to this change. What push-back and concerns might she have? What behaviors might she exhibit?

e. You can choose to do this exercise with a partner. You can speak from the perspective of the stakeholder and ask your partner to observe you. Do this for a few to several minutes.

5. Exit that embodied practice, shake it off for 30 seconds.

a. You can walk around a bit, shake your arms out, or whatever your Body needs to do to exit the embodied exercise.

6. With the unique insight of having been in her Body and knowing her reactions, push-back and concerns, how might you go about this change initiative?

a. What small tweaks may be helpful in making the change initiative more successful?

Note: This exercise "Put on Their Body" can be applicable not only for leading change initiatives, it can be used whenever you are trying to better understand someone else's perspective, or you want to exercise more empathy with someone.

DOING

**Embodied Actions
Elevate the OUTER GAME**

8

INTRODUCTION TO *DOING*

Introduction to DOING

We are what we repeatedly do. Excellence, then, is not an act, but a habit.[1] Aristotle

While our "inner game" is crucial and embodied self-awareness helps us up our "inner game", it needs to manifest in an "outer game" – i.e. real actions and observable behaviors - that allows us to connect with, influence, and inspire others. Excellence is a habit.

As stated by Harvard Business Review, American companies spend enormous amounts of money on employee training and education - $160 billion in the United States and close to $356 billion globally in 2015 alone, but learning does not lead to better organizational performance because people soon revert to their old ways of doing things.[2] Based on data from the Association for Talent Development, corporate working professionals often apply only about 15% of what they learn in many corporate training and development programs.[3]

Our desire for change usually does not translate into sustainable behavior change. Most of the time, leaders know intellectually and conceptually what they want to change, but then they struggle to embody it.

Integrating effective coaching with corporate training significantly increases the ROI of corporate dollars on learning and development. According to Forbes, a global survey of coaching clients by PriceWaterhouseCoopers and the Association Resource center concluded that the mean ROI for companies investing in coaching was seven times the initial investment, with over a quarter reporting an ROI of 10 to 49 times."[4]

In my experience, integrating coaching with training works well; but better yet, an integrative Mind-Body approach helps leaders maximize and accelerate their desired results. In the book "Leadership Embodiment," co-author Janet Crawford states that the vast majority of our behaviors and our decisions are determined before the thoughts hit our conscious minds.[5] In a similar vein, author and thought leader Doug Silsbee notes that we store in our tissues (our Body) the default habits that form our identity.[6]

The reality is, "The issue is in the tissue."[7]

If behavior patterns and habits are stored in our Body, how can we access our full intelligence and capacity of our Body and Mind to help drive desired change? How can we move from embodied awareness to embodied actions?

By tuning into our Body – a resource that is always with us – we can accelerate change by transforming desired actions to embodied actions. In fact, our Body is the most reliable vehicle to real action and is a secret accelerator to behavior change.

In Chapters 9-12, you will hear my own story and stories of other leaders who were able to establish desired leadership habits at the DOING level through embodied actions, which led to faster change and more sustainable growth.

THE
ISSUE
IS
IN
THE
TISSUE

9

EMBODIED ACTIONS TRANSFORM *IMPULSE CONTROL*

Embodied Actions Transform Impulse Control

Any person capable of angering you becomes your master. He can anger you only when you permit yourself to be disturbed by him.[1] *Epictetus*

We discussed the critical importance of emotional intelligence in leadership effectiveness and organizational results. For leaders at top tiers, Emotional intelligence accounts for nearly 90% of the difference between average and star performers.[2] Companies who have executives with higher levels of emotional intelligence are more likely to be highly profitable.[3]

A key component of emotional intelligence is self-regulation – emotionally and behaviorally.

Any high-achieving individual carries inside them passion and excitement. A certain emotional charge is part of what drives us and has helped us advance. The flipside of this charge can be a lack of control over undesirable emotions and behaviors. If left unchecked, we can alienate others and damage our ability to achieve the desired outcomes for ourselves and for our organizations.

Sometimes leaders receive feedback that they are too defensive or "blow up" too easily, or they tend to cut other people off when talking, or they tend to jump in to solve the problem themselves instead of empowering their team members to do so. Often, we have the best intent and desire to make a positive change, but real change is hard to achieve and difficult to sustain.

We are working with conditioned behavior patterns developed earlier on in our experiences and reinforced over a long period of time. According to emotional intelligence guru Daniel Goleman, "Our emotions are driven by biological impulses."[4] We are acting on an urge or impulse that is stored in our neurophysiology. It is a conditioned patterning, a neuro-muscular memory that overpowers our cognitive intent and bypasses our logical thinking.

Because of this intricate and undeniable Mind-Body connection, self-regulation and impulse control can be more easily accessed when we can tap into the intelligence of our Body and tune into our sensations at a physical level.

I would like to share a humbling personal experience in learning self-regulation and impulse control in managing my temper – a behavior change I was only able to access once I was able to identify it in my Body. This story is an example of deepening insight through embodied awareness and accelerating change through embodied actions.

Story
"I Hate My Temper"

My throat tightened and my chest was compressed. My blood flow was speeding up, pressure inside my veins building, like a jet of water ready to gush out of a fire hydrant. I could even feel it rushing up to my brain, a slight headache announcing the escalation. My eyes lost focus; my vocal cords seemed out of reach.

It felt extremely fast like lightning and extremely slow like slow-motion in a movie. Everything seemed to stop in that precise second.

Most distinctive in that moment was a tingling sensation on the outside of my arms, climbing up to my shoulders. This sensation was entirely new to my awareness.

In 2016, I was struggling with a temper, not in a professional setting, but with my daughter (who was 10 at that time) and sometimes with my husband. It was quite shocking for the rational part of me to analyze how I could be so professional at work, and yet so easily lose it with my loved ones. Yelling without warning, sometimes working myself up to a point of hyperventilation and full-body tremor, followed by intense internal embarrassment and shame for days, which would then build up more negative emotional charge, ready to explode upon the next trigger. I had been trying for several years to control my temper, without much success.

A few years before this, I went to a therapist for a few sessions, after I lost it on the day of my tenth wedding anniversary, triggered by something my husband said that I do not even remember. In the heat of emotions, I was ready to walk away from the marriage (all because of a trivial comment that I cannot even recall). This was my first experience with therapy, which helped me look back on my childhood.

My father is a very good man but he had an explosive temper. He was very physically abusive with one of my older brothers – the naughty one. It is a miracle that my brother survived. I never saw my father beat my mother physically, but there would be at least once or twice a day when he would smash a dinner plate onto the concrete floor in front of my mother, yelling and screaming. Throughout elementary school, middle school and high school, I would be hiding in my study room, mentally tense, not sure when I would hear that plate-smashing sound, so piercing and so constant that it was engraved into my conscious and unconscious landscape, a fragile little nervous system at that time.

So many years had passed and I had internally forgiven my father. I found peace with my past. There was something I did not realize until the therapy sessions. What I despised the most was what I had subconsciously picked up behaviorally now that I had my own child. The therapist suggested that even though I hated that temper behavior, it was my only experience with how to handle conflict with loved ones. Later, I learned that our Body, including our skeletal-muscular structure and our nervous system, carries and stores memories of our life and our conditioned response to our environment. Even though it had been many years since I left home, the embedded memory of violent reaction was triggered when I was in a situation of conflict with my loved ones.

I have the best daughter in the world. I had confessed to her in the past that Mom needs her help. Mom does not want to have this bad temper and Mom just does not know how to catch it to stop it. I told her that she is an amazing girl and there is nothing wrong with her. What triggered me were small things, such as when I told her multiple times to stop doing something and she still would not listen. She said she simply did not know that I was getting so close to being terribly upset. We discussed the idea of a signaling system.

One day, she came up with an idea for a signal.

"Mom," she said, "if you feel you have asked me to stop doing something multiple times and you are getting very upset, could you please tap on my right shoulder a few times, like a 'knock, knock', so I know that this is serious and I need to stop now?" I thought that was brilliant. I tried that with some success, but not enough.

At that time, I was going through professional coaching certification. Coaching is about bringing out the best in people and helping them achieve their desired outcomes through gaining awareness and implementing positive behavior change. I had to help myself first before I could help others. Managing my temper was on the top of my list. The most impactful part of my training is Body-Centered Coaching.[5]

All behavior patterns are habitual and physiological. To shift a habitual behavior, we need to first identify the biomarkers (biological markers) of our habitual patterns – the early warning signs of an urge at a physiological level. For a few months, I tried to catch those signs in my Body before my temper erupted. I tried diligently. Often, I was able to analyze it later, but I could not catch it quickly enough before the urge manifested into a behavior.

Until now.

I was leaning against the kitchen counter, my husband standing next to me. He said something that triggered me. My blood rushed, and very interestingly, I noticed the tingling on my outer arms climbing up to the shoulders.

For the very first time, in this crucial moment in my life, I was able to catch the distinct biomarkers of the warning signs before I acted out my temper.

I did not say a word. I quickly walked away from the kitchen, walked into the closet inside the master bedroom. It was a bit dark. I stood there. I breathed. I used my hands to brush down the tingling sensations on my outer arms, and I shook off my hands. I continued to breathe.

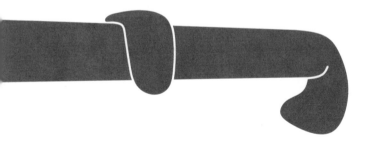

The intensity inside of me started to subside, mentally, emotionally, physically, in the nervous system distributed in my whole Body. Eventually I was completely calm – surprisingly calm, only several minutes after what felt like a heart attack. Arising from that calmness was a sense of power, a sense of control, a sense of empowerment. For the very first time, I was no longer a slave to my temper.

This experience reminds me of a famous quote by Viktor Frankl. "Between stimulus and response there is a space. In that space is our power to choose our response. In our response lies our growth and our freedom."[6] Through identifying the unique biomarkers associated with my temper, I was able to find the space between stimulus and response and I had the power to choose.

Between stimulus and response there is a space. In that space is our power to choose our response. In our response lies our growth and our freedom.

Viktor Frankl

Since that day in 2016, I have not had another episode of temper. I was able to deepen self-awareness in a highly embodied way and accelerate change to a desired calmer response. I was able to free myself from a deeply set habitual pattern and switch to a new level of awareness and action. It was the most profound behavior change I have experienced in my life, one that I had never thought was possible.

Leadership Lesson
Face It to Shift It

In the heat of an emotional reaction, there is little chance to change an old habit intellectually. In his book *Emotional Intelligence: Why It Can Matter More Than IQ*, Daniel Goleman famously called such reactions an "amygdala hijack."[7]

According to noted neurologist Antonio R. Damasio, each event we store in our memories comes connected with a series of bodily sensations that we felt when we went through it for the first time.[8] He termed these bodily sensations as "somatic markers", which are referred to as biomarkers in this book.

We cannot change an impulse involving a physical response until we are aware of what is happening on the physiological level. To make a true positive change from stubborn old habits, it takes intentional effort to face the urge or impulse then to disrupt or shift it.

To face and disrupt a neuro-muscular memory, we need to be a detective, catching ourselves and paying attention to the detailed sensations in our Body – those relevant biomarkers. Sometimes we can catch them, sometimes not. That is normal. Overtime, we will be able to catch them more frequently and take action to bring ourselves back to a centered and desired state of self-regulation – in my case, my action was to breathe and to shake off my arms. We should celebrate every time we catch even the tiniest bit of sensation, and not beat ourselves up for not being successful at it.

PAY

ATTENTION

to
your

BODY

The next time you experience an undesired behavior impulse, pay attention to your Body. Try to see if you can find the accompanying physical sensations. What do you notice as you cut someone off or as you get angry? Does your Body lean forward? Does your chest tighten? Do you feel any tension around your throat? Do your legs become restless? What happens with your eye gaze? Ask for feedback from those you trust. They see your behaviors more clearly than you see yourself.

Embodied Leadership Practice
Catch the Impulse Biomarkers

1. Think of a moment when you did not exercise desired impulse control and jumped into a habitual behavior instead. Put on that Body and try to feel the sensations in that moment. Capture a list of physical sensations as biomarkers. Put a checkmark for each time you catch any of the sensations. You can use Table 2 as a template.

   a. It may be challenging to do so in the beginning. It does not need to be a comprehensive or good list. Your skill on this will build as you pay more attention to your physical sensations overtime.

   b. For example, my biomarkers before I used to burst into temper were throat and chest tightening, blood flow speeding up, slight headache building, eyes losing focus, vocal cords seeming out of reach, and tingling sensation on the outside of my arms climbing up to my shoulders.

2. In the next few weeks, notice any similar impulses. Pay attention to those specific biomarkers you have captured above. Be a detective and catch these sensations.

   a. Do not try to change anything, just notice.

   b. You can use Table 2 to capture your wins as a detective.

c. Celebrate each time you catch these biomarkers.

3. Allow yourself to notice what happens. Keep practicing. Make being a detective fun and give yourself a small prize when you make progress.

  a. Once you can catch yourself in action, take a second to breathe and to choose your desired action. You may realize that "noticing" alone can shift the stubborn impulse, because your attention is directed towards "noticing" hence away from acting out the impulse itself. You are gaining yourself that precious micro-moment between stimulus and response – the space for your power to choose.

TABLE 2

Biomarkers	Day 1	Day 2	Day 3	Day 4	Day 5	Day 6	Day 7
1							
2							
3							
4							

10

EMBODIED ACTIONS ENABLE

POWERFUL
LISTENING

115

Embodied Actions Enable Powerful Listening

The sea is lower and quieter than all streams, hence it is the grandest of all.[1]

Lao Tzu

Our culture has placed disproportional emphasis on speaking as compared to listening. Often, we focus on advocating our ideas and viewpoints instead of listening to others or inquiring into their perspectives. Sometimes we may be quiet, but we are not really actively listening to the speaker's emotions or intent; hence we do not truly understand, let alone empathize, in order to serve the conversation in a meaningful way.

In his best-selling book T*he 7 Habits of Highly Effective People*, Stephen Covey named Habit 5 as "seek first to understand, then to be understood."[2] Kenneth Blanchard and Spencer Johnson, authors of *The One Minute Manager*, assert that the best way to engage employees is to allocate time to listen to employees.[3] 97% of 500,000 leaders and consultants surveyed said that they believe listening to their employees and incorporating their ideas is critical to an organization's success.[4]

The quality of our leadership largely depends on our ability to communicate effectively. The quality of our communication largely depends on our ability to actively listen. People cannot hear us until they are heard. Being fully listened to and being truly heard is probably one of the best gifts anyone can receive. With increasing amount of stimulus around us and our relentless focus on efficiency, active listening is not easy and requires intentional effort.

We can learn and establish a new behavior pattern and embody our desired actions by creating new associations between our Body and Mind. This is supported by "What fires together, wires together"[5], a phrase coined by Canadian neuroscientist Donald Hebb - now known as Hebb's law. In the context of embodied actions accelerating real change, once the new association between the Body and Mind is established and repeated, a desired new habit is formed.

WHAT FIRES TOGETHER, WIRES TOGETHER *Donald Hebb*

By engaging in a new pattern anchored on an embodied action or a physical practice, we can disrupt old habits and acquire new skills such as active listening and being present in the moment.

Story
"I Can't Quiet My Mind to Listen"

Tom was the General Manager of a metals distribution division in a large global company. Tom had a healthy tan on his face, as if he had just walked off a golf course. He is always well-composed and positive. Nothing gets him down. He is a strong leader, and he wants to be able to better engage and empower his team for accelerated business results.

During one of our coaching conversations, Tom mentioned he could not quiet his mind to listen to his direct reports, because his brain is turning so fast. While others are still talking, he has already understood the point and solved their problem, perhaps even two additional problems that have not yet even been brought up. It shows in his body language. People sense his impatience and have provided this feedback to him. When acting in this habitual pattern, he shared that he felt unanchored and a sense of un-ease in his Body.

Tom wanted to be able to anchor himself better, so that he could actively listen to his team members and be present in the conversations, which would help him to be better engaged with his team.

We were meeting in a conference center. We sat at a small round table, draped with a crisp, white tablecloth, and decorated with fresh flowers for the day.

I asked Tom how he normally has discussions with his direct

reports - sitting or standing. Typically, he would be sitting, his right leg crossed over his left knee. He modeled this as he spoke.

I noticed that his right knee was touching the bottom of the small round table.

While Tom was in that position, I asked, "If your Body had its own intelligence, what would it tell you to do right now to anchor in this position?"

Both intrigued and perplexed, Tom paused for a second, looking at me – checking that I was serious. Then he turned his attention inward to himself and his Body, contemplative. I smiled and nodded to honor his trust in my invitation.

"I can push my right knee up against the table," Tom said after a few seconds. "It pushes the rest of my Body down towards the chair and the floor. I think that can help to anchor me."

"I see!" I acknowledged his connection with his Body.

Tom stayed in this explorative mode, focused; the freshly starched white tablecloth draped over his leg.

"If it gets really bad, I can also push the palms of my two hands up against the bottom of the table, it gives me three points of contact with the table which will further anchor my body."

I invited Tom to try that out again in the moment, and to really identify and locate the anchoring sensations in his Body.

Tom reported that this physical practice of anchoring automatically caused him to drop his energy down towards the ground, his sitting posture shifted back slightly toward his chair from a forward-leaning position. I could also feel that he lowered his breathing from his chest to his belly, and the pace of his breathing slowed down as he spoke. His gaze softened, more focused on me, and less restless than before.

Anchor Your Listening Body

Tom stayed in that moment a little while longer, to lock in what he was noticing in his sensations. The aroma of the fresh flowers on the table gently brushed my nose as I also took a few deep relaxing breaths with Tom.

Tom's body language indicated that he was energized by this practice, and he said he was ready to give this practice a try over the next two weeks.

The next time I saw Tom, he was beaming within his healthy golfer tan.

"The knee-up-against-the-table thing really works!" he said.

"It's still hard and I don't always catch myself. But I can pull myself out of the old habit of racing ahead. I can bring myself to the present moment and listen to the other person much better."

Tom was happy that not only he, but also his team, had started to notice a difference, except his team did not know his secret. He asked me how I knew something like this could work. I told him jokingly that it was my "ancient Chinese secret."

Leadership Lesson
Be Here and Now

I often reference Tom's story of enhancing listening presence through the Body, because it is a simple example of a challenge to which many people can relate. The embodied action or physical practice is always best when organically developed with the individual leader, so it differs from person to person.

In Tom's case, he first noticed his habitual urge to race forward. He created an embodied action or a physical practice to anchor his Body so he can be "here and now", which led to an emotional state of calmness and centeredness. He also intentionally associated that psycho-physiological state with a cognitive intent to actively listen. Remember, cells that fire together, wire together.[5] Over time, this embodied action of anchoring the Body and the thought of listening became wired together, and a new habit is formed.

After noticing our existing behavior patterns at a physical level, we can invite the Body to help us come up with a simple embodied action or physical practice. Disrupt the old habit by developing a new and desired behavior pattern. It becomes more and more natural with practice over time.

Trust the intelligence of the Body. As part of our decision-making process, our brain takes in sensory input from both interior and exterior senses. Our Body is part of our "distributed brain"[6] and therefore is part of our integrated intelligence. Why rely on one singular tool when we can access a whole basket of tools?

Trust Your Body - Your Distributed Brain

Embodied Leadership Practice
Anchor Your Listening Body

1. Bring back a memory when you were not being an active listener. Put yourself in that moment now. Notice your urge to speak. Where does that urge reside in your Body? Break it down. Be specific.

   a. In my case, when I get into my "driver" mode and want to solve the problem and get to the results quickly without actively listening, my upper Body tends to lean forward, my facial muscles become just a bit restless, my mouth wants to open, my tongue wants to move, my hands are not relaxed, my eyes start to wander a bit instead of being focused on my conversation partner. I feel a bubbly sensation inside my chest, and my upper shoulders tense up.

2. Think of an upcoming conversation and set an intention to be a powerful listener.

   a. It can be a conversation with a specific person in a specific situation that could trigger you to not be an ideal listener.

3. Decide in advance one way to use your Body to help you anchor.

   a. Follow your in-the-moment intuition. You cannot

be wrong. You can always tweak it and change it based on what feels right.

b. Some examples that my clients and I have experimented with are: feeling the Body firmly supported by the chair; feeling all four corners of the feet firmly planted on the ground; pushing the back slightly against the chair; pushing both palms down on the chair; pushing up one knee against the bottom of the table (as in Tom's story); pressing the tongue up against the roof of the mouth; pushing thumbs against each other; pressing the nails, etc. The sky is the limit – well, your Body is the limit. You can come up with a hundred ways and cannot be wrong.

4. Practice anchoring using what you came up with in Step 3.

a. While you experiment with this anchoring practice, you can also incorporate Steps 3 and 4 in the Embodied Leadership Practice included at the end of Chapter 6.

b. Practice multiple times a day (it takes less than 1 minute each time) so that such anchoring becomes more readily recruitable through your Body when needed. Much like in sports, we practice a skill before we need to use it in a game.

c. Reflect on what worked well and what can be tweaked at the end of each day. You may find it helpful to invite an accountability partner.

5. When you are in the actual conversation mentioned in Step 2, practice your choice of physical anchoring.

   a. Allow it to be fluid and allow your sensations and feelings to guide you, follow what feels good and grounding.

6. As you anchor yourself and listen, try to listen to the emotions of your conversation partner. Try to listen to the intent behind the words. Acknowledge their viewpoints and even their emotions (for example, "That must have been frustrating for you.")

Remember, people cannot hear you until they are heard. The best gift you can give to someone is to make her feel heard like she has never been heard before. Powerful listening begets powerful ability to engage and influence others, and to obtain critical buy-in needed in leadership.

11
EMBODIED ACTIONS FACILITATE

THINKING & ACTING STRATEGICALLY

Embodied Actions Facilitate
Thinking & Acting Strategically

Your vision rises when you are standing on higher ground.[1] *Chinese Proverb*

As high-performing leaders, we need to continuously hone our skills in strategic thinking and in turning our vision into strategic actions. As leaders and leadership coaches, it is also our job to help others think and act strategically. As dancers on the stage of leadership, we need to be able to be on the dance floor (taking actions) and on the balcony (doing strategic thinking) at the same time.

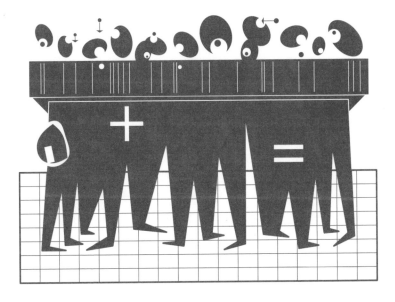

On the Dance Floor AND the Balcony

In a survey of 10,000 senior leaders by Management Research Group (MRG), 97% of them said that being strategic was the leadership behavior most important to their organization's success.[2] A survey by Roger Martin of the Rotman School of Management found that 67% of managers believe their organization is bad at developing strategy.[3]

So, how can we become more strategic leaders and how can we help other leaders become more strategic in their thinking and actions?

There are many articles on this topic, and most of them focus on the Mind. Often, leaders know conceptually they should be more strategic but fail to have true understanding of the gap; or they have a solid self-awareness of the gap but fail to turn that awareness into actions. Remember we discussed in Chapter 9 the "biological impulses" as drivers of emotions and the importance of working with "biomarkers" or "somatic markers" in behavior change and habit building?

We can help leaders accelerate positive change in behavior and thinking patterns by tapping into the holistic intelligence of the Body and Mind. First, we need to help them gain embodied awareness of how they tend to show up, how being strategic makes a difference, and how they have the power within them to be strategic. From there, we can support them on developing a desired new habit by practicing embodied actions related to thinking and acting strategically.

I typically facilitate Experiential Coaching in a creative setting outside of a traditional work environment. I invite the leader or the leadership team to choose a creative venue based on their interest, so they can have some fun while learning about themselves. As we observe and learn about any behavior pattern - which typically reflects a particular underlying thinking pattern, we can gain powerful in-the-moment embodied awareness, and shift to a new way of BEING. This type of embodied insight deepens the leader's awareness and conviction for a positive change – such as thinking and acting strategically.

The story below illustrates how a leader explored embodied awareness ("BEING") in an art museum to help her step back for a more strategic view, and designed embodied actions ("DOING") to help her get "out of her head and onto her feet."

Story

"How Do I Get Out of My Head and Just Do It"

I had the pleasure to coach Melissa, the Vice President of Service Delivery at a fast-growing engineering and construction firm. She was in her early forties wearing large eyeglasses that suited her well. Shoulder-length curly hair clung to her cheeks, yet never covered the contagious enthusiasm on her face.

Melissa's department touched everyone in the business, from pre-sale to post-sale. With the company's significant market expansion, the work of her team became more and more important to the company's ability to execute its aggressive growth plans.

One of Melissa's coaching goals was to lead more strategically. Part of her challenge was her perfectionist tendency and fear of failure or disappointment. When it came to something important, she found herself procrastinating and not taking the first step, which hindered her ability to take strategic actions.

In the middle of our six-month coaching engagement, Melissa accepted my invitation to an Experiential Coaching session. She picked the venue. She likes art and it had been sometime since she had visited MOCA (Museum of Contemporary Art) Cleveland, one of city's architectural icons, so her choice was easy.

After entering the unusually shaped building through its

revolving front door, we sat down on a colorful curved bench on the first floor.

We discussed what Melissa was interested in exploring, an inquiry or question she would like to get more clarity on. Melissa said, "How do I get out of my head and just do it when it comes to strategic items? How do I make my feet do what my head already knows"?

I said I would hold her inquiry for her, so she could put it aside and enjoy the art museum.

The stairs up to the higher floors were designed as part of the architectural and artistic experience, inviting our eyes to new pieces of art at every corner we turned. On the second floor, we went through a commanding floor-to-ceiling steel-and-glass door into a big open space, which featured an exhibit named "Sunday Paintings" by Byron Kim.

The artist captured a portrait of the sky every Sunday for 49 weeks. The 49 uniform canvas pieces were hung consecutively on three different walls. On each piece, some writing in a tiny font described the mood of that particular Sunday.

Melissa first walked close to a few pieces facing her as she walked in, examining the details of each. She studied the writing on the pieces for a while and commented on her intrigue. I saw her eyes growing bigger behind her round eyeglasses. She was captivated by the words on the canvases.

As I noticed her first reaction to examine the details, I invited her to take a step back and see what she would notice.

As she did, her head tilted to the side and her eyes taking in the art. She said she noticed a shift in what she was seeing.

"OK?" I invited gently.

She no longer saw the writing on each piece, she was able to see a theme in the artist's color palette – various shades of blues against a white background. She noticed how the portrait of the sky changed from one piece to the next, ever so slightly.

Keeping the distance from the art pieces, Melissa slowly walked along the walls, appreciating the sky of progressing Sundays. I walked slowly behind her to give her some space to experience the art.

At the end of one wall of Sunday paintings, I asked Melissa, "I wonder what it would be like if you took an even bigger step back and stood right in the middle of the room?"

She tried, intrigued. We were the only patrons in the space at this time.

Melissa was as still as the Sunday paintings on the walls. Her facial muscles relaxed, her shoulders settled, and her lower Body grounded. I almost felt a light breeze brushing through the blue and white skies on the walls. I took a calm deep breath. From several feet away, I could feel the slowing of her breathing.

Melissa was scanning all three walls, appreciating the entire exhibit as one big and integral piece of art. I could tell insights were emerging in her.

Eventually, Melissa came up to me, ready to debrief. She had a lot to share, without any prompts.

"I stepped back and looked up!" Her eyes beamed. She sounded like a kid who has just discovered a new toy, full of aliveness.

"I was able to see the whole picture, not just the pieces. It's a totally different view!"

I asked how this might be relevant to her inquiry for the day - "How do I get out of my head and just do it? How do I make my feet do what my head already knows"?

"I just need to 'look up' once in a while." Her answer came naturally.

I just need to 'look up' once in a while.

Melissa realized that she did not always have to be consumed by the details or try to make every detail perfect, simply because she was good at it. As a more senior leader, she can take a step back to see the bigger picture - a global view – and be more strategic.

Melissa was not speaking just from her Mind on a conceptual level. Instead, she had a direct and immersive experience in her Body of what it was like to take a big step back (literally) and to experience a shift in what she saw, sensed, and felt in a way that was fully alive.

Touched and inspired by her insights, I was glad that our art experience had helped her gain embodied awareness. Sometimes all it takes to break through the stuck-ness is a change of scenery gaining powerful insight through a felt experience.

But there is more.

Melissa proceeded to share her second insight: the simplicity of the possible.

"All the artist needed to create something this amazing," she began, "were small canvases, brushes, paint, and a pen."

"When he started to paint on the first Sunday, Byron may not have known how this project would ever turn out. He just trusted himself to get started. He must have trusted that once he got started, at some point down the road, the right curator would be there to co-create a vision of how to display and install the art pieces in a museum."

I was quiet, but actively listening and fully present. I felt a sense of an opening, an expansion within the space where we stood, like light cracking through clusters of clouds. I found myself taking another deep breath, curious where Melissa would take her new insight.

"I don't need to have the final answer before getting started!" Melissa was on a roll. Melissa said that she realized her tendency to get hung up on getting all the details perfect which results in procrastinating on important and strategic items. The insight from the artist creating a major work of art with just a few very simple items gave her the inspiration to get out of her head and just do it, and to make her feet do what her head already knows to do!

Our energies joined in celebrating her moment of insights. The sun was fully out of the clouds in the sky, I could even hear birds singing.

As we were getting ready to leave the room, I asked Melissa if I could share an observation. I had noticed that she had the ability to attend to the details, and she was comfortable stepping back to see the big picture, drawing strategic insights. She can toggle between the two.

Melissa blushed a bit, then admitted she was not good at giving herself credit. Then, slowly and thoughtfully, she shared yet a third insight.

"My toolbox has everything I need already! I do not need to have all the answers to get started. It's OK to be easy with myself, and I can do it!"

Her voice became deeper and more resonant, her Body was anchored with a sense of conviction, a big smile on her face, which conveyed self-confidence – the kind of confidence rooted in the ground and rising up through the entire Body. Her energy carried power.

Before we left the museum, Melissa came up with a physical practice (an embodied action) – a sequence of arm movements and breathing that looks like a modified version of a sun salutation in yoga. She literally takes a step back, physically raises her head to look up while opening and sweeping up her arms from both sides, takes a breath, then brings down her arms in front of her sending energy to her feet. She decided to practice this physical sequence several times a day.

My toolbox has everything I need already!

Associated with this embodied action (Body) and associated feelings of confidence is a thinking narrative (Mind) to be more strategic and to put thoughts into action. The sequence was designed as a daily reminder to be strategic, to step back, to look up, and to "get out of the head and just do it".

Over the course of six months, Melissa's stakeholders observed a measurable positive change in her strategic leadership, as they enthusiastically shared in the mini survey at the end of our coaching program.

Leadership Lesson
"Move" to Strategic Actions

Embodied learning deepens self-awareness, embodied actions accelerate real change.

In the story of Melissa, she gained embodied awareness of how she has an orientation for details and perfection, how taking a step back and looking up makes a big difference, and how she already has the tools to act strategically. With that embodied awareness, she proceeded to design a simple embodied action to remind her to be centered, to take a step back and to look up, and to get out of her head and just do it.

It is important to tie the desired new behavior (acting strategically) to an embodied action or physical practice to make the behavior change anchored, accessible, and lasting. Cells that fire together wire together.[4] A deliberate embodied action can call up the desired behavior and associated emotions and thoughts through repeated practice.

Giving feedback on her Experiential Coaching session, Melissa said her direct immersive experience at MOCA Cleveland was much more impactful than just talking about the topic on a conceptual level. "It feels very personal, specific and very tailored." A year later, Melissa told me that she still practices her physical movement as a reminder to think and act strategically.

Embodied Leadership Practice
Step Back and Look Up

1. Think of something or someone that brings you calmness and joy. Allow your Body to be open and relaxed.

2. Visualize being a strategic thinker who can see far and wide. Notice any subtle movements in your Body and exaggerate it to a bigger scale movement.

   a. If you are not able to notice any natural subtle physical movement, then simply make up a small movement that would mean "being strategic" to you. As a default, you can try taking a small step back with your legs and raising your head to look up.

   b. For example, when I think of being strategic, my spine straightens up and I feel taller, my head and upper body shift from a slightly forward disposition back to a more neutral position in line with my spine. My shoulders open, and I take a deeper breath at the same time. Sometimes when I think of being strategic, I feel like lifting up to my tippy toes and raising one hand by my forehead as if trying to look far ahead.

3. Practice this simple movement a few times a day for the next few weeks.

a. Allow your Body to guide you. If you feel like switching to a different movement the next day, that is OK. Go with what feels right to you.

b. Once you land with a desired physical practice, stick with it to allow yourself to build some "muscle memory" (Mind-Body association).

4. As you practice this simple physical movement and think about being strategic, notice any positive emotions that come up as you practice. Hold and carry these positive emotions with you as you go about your day.

5. Reflect daily on how you have been able to think and act strategically. Celebrate your tiny wins and tweak your actions as appropriate.

12
EMBODIED
ACTIONS
MAKE
DELEGATION
REAL

Embodied Actions Make
Delegation Real

*A masterful leader does very little, yet
little is left undone.*[1] Lao Tzu

The famous former CEO of GE Jack Welch said that "Before
you are a leader, success is all about growing yourself. When
you become a leader, success is all about growing others."[2] As
leaders, we achieve desired results with and through others.

Most of us started our careers as individual contributors and
we have achieved much success with our ability to efficiently
solve problems and execute plans. As stated in the title of the
book by Marshall Goldsmith, *What got you here won't get you
there.*[3] Delegation is a crucial skill for any leader who wants to
take on more responsibilities and elevate her impact.

Even though we know our career trajectory and our professional
impact is largely affected by our ability to delegate, it is difficult
to overcome our habitual pattern of doing things ourselves.
We have practiced jumping into doing things so much that it
has become a habit, like an automatic pilot. According to Dan
Siegel, psychiatry professor, author, and creator of the field
of Interpersonal Neurobiology, automatic pilot is "reflected in
reactive and enduring patterns of thought and bodily posture
and movement, in which the past is shaping present perceptual
biases, emotional responses, and behavioral output."[4]

Because our behavior patterns are so deeply engrained in our neurophysiology as automatic reactions, it is exceedingly difficult to change those well-practiced habits by just thinking of the desired change in our Mind alone. If the challenge resides in our physical reaction, it is time that we tackle it at a physical level.

The following story demonstrates the power of working with the Body through embodied actions, where a coaching client designed an embodied action or physical practice to develop a new habit of effective delegation.

Story

"How Do I Delegate If I Can Do it Faster?"

I was hired to coach the head of support operations, John, at a large retail chain of luxury goods. John is brilliant, passionate, and an amazing problem solver. One of the development areas John focused on was effective delegation.

John and I worked together for nine months. Our coaching conversations first focused on discovery and gaining self-awareness. Yes, you guessed it correctly, he developed embodied awareness through an experiential coaching session - at the local botanical garden. As we shifted our focus from awareness to actions in the second half of our engagement, we started to explore embodied actions.

One day, we were exploring how to better delegate to his team. John is extremely good at what he does. He has a tremendous workload and it seemed much easier for him to just do the work and solve the problems himself. In fact, it has become a habit.

John's question was, "How do I delegate if I can do it myself faster?"

I asked him about his typical physical reaction when thinking about, facing, and taking on new work tasks.

He said, every morning, the first thing he does in the office is to go to his computer and start tackling the issues in his inbox. He was moving his hands in a typing motion while he was talking to me. In a rigid posture, his full Body was in a "head-on attack" mode in front of his computer.

I appreciated the physical modeling of his behavior pattern. I explained to him the power of embodied actions and the neuroscience behind it (what fires together wires together)[5], and how the Body is a key passageway to positive behavior change.

I invited him to recruit his Body's intelligence. When I asked him about something his Body could do to remind him to delegate, he said he was game.

We played with it a bit. He came up with a small sequence of physical moves. He decided to do them every morning when he came to his office - before he started typing on the computer keyboard and attacking the tasks and problems himself.

First, he extends his arms out in front of his chest with palms away from him, he takes a deep breath in while he brings both arms up and palms in towards his chest and while straightening his spine, he would then exhale and bring his palms down pushing both arms out away from himself in front of his chest.

I asked him what this small sequence of movement meant to him in the context of what we were working on.

John explained it as follows:

"When I hold out my arms out in front of me, I am pausing and not going to the computer. As I bring arms and hands in and take a few breaths, I am reminding myself to take everything in, not just react. When I sit up tall with a straight spine, I am reminding myself to think and act more strategically. After taking a moment to process what is coming at me, I push my hands out, which makes me intentionally think about delegating work to my team, rather than rushing to do it myself."

I always marvel at what clients come up with. When we are open and willing to tap into our full intelligence, it is amazing to see the creativity that blossoms.

At the end of the coaching program, John's stakeholders unanimously reported measurable improvement in his ability to delegate which was critical to the success of his team and the company.

Leadership Lesson
Less Is More

As a leader with ever greater responsibilities and an increasing number of team members, how we delegate effectively underpins our ability to achieve our desired results. Effective leaders focus their energy on the critical few things that ONLY they can do.

Less is more. Delegation is a must. But change is hard.

Journalist and best-selling author A.J. Jacobs notes that "It is easier to act your way into a new thinking, than to think your way into a new way of acting."[6]

> # It is easier to act your way into a new thinking, than to think your way into a new way of acting.
>
> A.J. Jacobs

In the story of John, he established and practiced embodied actions – taking a breath and evaluating incoming tasks, straightening his spine to be strategic, then pushing his arms out as a reminder to delegate work to others.

A key for any leader in leading a team is to practice the act of delegation, and to embody this intention behaviorally. You too can design and experiment with a small embodied action to help you develop a desired habit in delegation.

Play, be creative, let your Body inform you. Do not overthink it. Smile!

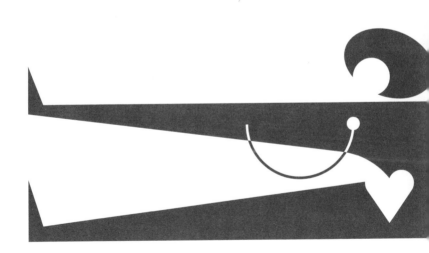

Embodied Leadership Practice
Act Your Way into Delegation

1. Relax. Think about the benefits associated with better delegation.

    a. Allow your Body to feel free. Maybe go somewhere else instead of your office. Maybe put on your favorite music. Or perhaps it is right here, right now.

2. As you invite your Body to inform you of a simple physical movement or posture that means delegation to you.

    a. Give yourself 30 seconds or less.

    b. If you do not like what you came up with, change it.

    c. In John's case, his simple physical movement was to extend his arms out in front of his chest, pull them in towards his chest then push them out to the front. This movement meant "take it in, process it, and push it out" or delegation to John.

3. Try it on for a few times, tweak it as you desire, but no more than 1-2 minutes. Land on something without over-thinking it.

    a. You can tweak it anytime.
    b. No one can judge you on how good or bad this practice is.

4. Practice this simple movement several times a day for the next few weeks.

   a. Tweak it as you or your Body desires.

   b. It takes little time – may be 30 seconds each time.

   c. As you practice this physical movement, bring up the feeling of freedom (or any other positive feeling you associate with the results of delegation) and think about the idea of delegation - your mental narrative could be "delegation" or "I am a good delegator" or something else that positively affirms delegation.

5. Reflect at the end of each day on what you did well and what you may tweak the next day about delegation. Practice again the next day and make it fun!

6. It's always a good idea to seek feedback from people around you when you are developing new and desired leadership behaviors. Recruit a few "support buddies" whom you trust and can give you timely and honest feedback and suggestions. This applies to all leadership practices included in this book.

INVITATION
NEW POSSIBILITIES

INVITATION
New Possibilities

Nothing is impossible, the word itself says, 'I'm possible!'[1] Audrey Hepburn

Even with the best intentions and the hardest work, leaders find it difficult to make measurable behavior changes to create effective long-term growth. For those of us who are tied of the same old tools and are interested in creative yet proven ways to achieve better leadership results, an integrative Mind-Body approach in Embodied Leadership is a better and more effective tool. Embodied Leadership helps us up our game, make meaningful impact, while feeling whole.

In this book, you have seen that both BEING ("inner game", or "how we choose to be") and DOING ("outer game", or "what we choose to do") involve the wholeness of our Body and Mind.

In BEING, embodied awareness helps us get attuned to our present-moment physical, emotional, and mental states and become aware of our conditioned responses to the world around us. It deepens our awareness and conviction for a desired positive change.

In DOING, embodied actions invite our Body as a trusted resource to help us build desired new habits. With embodied actions, we accelerate real change and hone our ability to make intentional choices to create the self and world that we desire.

Together, embodied BEING and DOING help us achieve accelerated results and sustained growth.

Through the various case studies in this book, you have seen practical applications of Embodied Leadership in addressing real-life leadership challenges. Exploring the integration of Mind and Body, leaders learned to connect with their authentic self, develop emotional intelligence, enhance executive presence, drive change, learn impulse control, listen powerfully, think and act strategically, and lead through delegation. This book also offers several Embodied Leadership Practices that you can put into use right away and share with those whom you care about and wish to support.

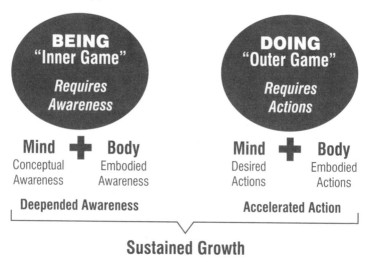

Life is an inside job. Leadership is an inside job.

Look beneath the surface. Go inward to your source. Look beyond the surface waves and go into the depth of the ocean.

There, at our core, at our home, accessed and anchored through our Body – the temple of our soul, we go back to our most powerful and resourceful self, we unlock our power from within.

Find the Deep Quietness of the Ocean

There, we can choose to align what we think, feel, speak, and do to be true to who we are, without wasting unnecessary energy due to lack of congruence.

There, we do not need to just DO more or work harder. We can choose and shift how we want to BE.

From there, DOING becomes much more effortless, focused, and effective. Leadership is authentic and inspiring. Life is whole and fulfilling.

It is my hope that you connect with your inner power from the alignment of your Mind and Body. From that place of congruence, you enjoy the pleasure of expressing life in an original and courageous way that inspires others around you, who then inspire many others around them.

We can all make a difference, in making leadership more filled with life, and in making life more worth living.

Welcome to a new world of possibilities!

ACKNOWLEDGMENTS

This book is my labor of love, supported by the love of an amazing team.

I am grateful to my long-time mentor Craig Arnold who advised me to "stay authentic" because I have "a unique approach", to John Andrica who offered generous support and has expanded my horizon over 20 years, to Stan Mickens who taught me the most about leadership, to Siisi Adu-Gyamfi who has been an unwavering guide, to Nelda Connors who models the elegance of a female executive, and to Rita Brauneck who has been a wonderful mentor since I started coaching.

I am grateful for the trust bestowed on me and this book by Stewart Kohl, Randy McShepard, Brett Lindsey, Steve Kessen, Sean Wenger, Erik Weyls, Lawrence McFadden, Lakisha Miller-Barclay, Dr. Serpil Erzurum, and Jennifer van Dijk.

I want to thank Melvin Smith for his unbelievable guidance throughout the book project, Marshall Goldsmith for his encouragement to write the book, and Richard Boyatzis for his candid feedback that launched me into many rounds of editing that made the book far better.

I want to thank my developmental editor Nicolas Gattig who helped me efficiently develop the structure and content of the first draft, Jack Bialosky who painstakingly edited the book line by line with precision, Hallie Crouch who generously lent her amazing eye for flow and her graceful expressions, Marc Manack, Kalli Vimr, Brent Ewing, and D. Greg Scott who helped me with content and title.

In the beginning stage of writing this book, my friend Helen Samson-Mullen suggested that I just write a "shitty first draft" when perfectionism was holding me back. My peer coach Betsy Ross' accountability check-ins helped me get the first round of stories down on paper quickly. Marcy Shankman shared her book-writing insights and encouragement. Lori Wald and I provided writing support to each other. JJ Digeronimo, Rita Montlack, and Leslie Yerkes shared their experiences with publishers. As I refined the book, my friends Jin Yan, Yu Jian, Nikos Angelis, and Wa'il Selfo wisely shared their perspectives on ancient Chinese, Greek, and Egyptian wisdom. Jonathan Reitz, Kevin Weaver, Sri Rahm, Fran Belkin, John Voso, and Jim Smith helped me explore printing options. Amy Guth generously shared post-publishing advice. Katherine Friedell, Mary Lynn Laughlin, Cindy Schultz, and Jonathan Vinocur are sounding boards I counted on. Eric Eichhorn helped me understand how to make the book available on Amazon. Kellie Rotunno provided document management support. I appreciate Jing Lauengco who is an inspiration in speaking one's own voice, Brandi Larsen who masterful guided me on the self-publishing journey, and Ted Sikora who captured me in author photo and video.

One of the things that excited me the most about this book project is collaborating with the amazing designer Frank Jacobus who never seizes to blow my mind with his gift. He curated your visual experience of this book from cover to cover.

My parents and siblings in China encouraged me to pursue my dreams, my parents-in-law in the United States made me feel that I have found a home away from home. I could not have written this book without the unwavering support and love from my dear husband Robert and our fantastic daughter Siena. I had many moments of getting in the zone of writing or editing instead of being available for the family during 2020. They forgive me and stand by me. They are the anchor of my courage to be me.

NOTES

KEY TERMS

1. Alan Fogal, *Three States of Embodied Self-Awareness* (International Body Psychotherapy Journal - The Art and Science of Somatic Praxis, Volume 19, Number 1, Spring/Summer 2020, pp. 39-49); retrieved from https://www.ibpj.org/issues/articles/Alan%20Fogel%20-%20Three%20States%20of%20Embodied%20Self-Awareness.pdf

1 YOU

1. Lao Tzu - original Chinese name Lao Zi (551-479 BCE), *Dao De Jing* (often translated to English as *Tao Te Ching*), Chapter 33. This quote is translated to English by author.

2 THE POWER OF THE BODY IN LEADERSHIP

1. This Chinese proverb is translated to English by author.

2. Wendy Palmer, Janet Crawford, *Leadership Embodiment: How the Way We Sit and Stand Can Change the Way We Think and Speak* (CreateSpace Independent Publishing Platforms, 2013)

3. Alan Fogal, *Three States of Embodied Self-Awareness* (International Body Psychotherapy Journal - The Art and Science of Somatic Praxis, Volume 19, Number 1, Spring/Summer 2020, pp. 39-49); retrieved from https://www.ibpj.org/issues/articles/Alan%20Fogel%20-%20Three%20States%20of%20Embodied%20Self-Awareness.pdf

4. John C. Norcross, Marci S. Mrykalo, Matthew D. Blagys, Auld Lang Syne: *Success Predictors, Change Processes, and Self-Reported Outcomes of New Year's Resolvers and Non-resolvers* (Journal of Clinical Psychology, 58,4: 397-405, April 2002); retrieved from https://pubmed.ncbi.nlm.nih.gov/11920693/

5. Ron Ashkenas, *Change Management Needs to Change* (Harvard Business Review, April 2013); retrieved from https://hbr.org/2013/04/change-management-needs-to-cha

6. Charles Duhigg, *The Power of Habit; Duhigg's interview by NPR, captured in article Habits: How They Form And How To Break Them* (NPR, March 2012);

retrieved from https://www.npr.org/2012/03/05/147192599/habits-how-they-form-and-how-to-break-them

3 INTRODUCTION TO BEING

1. Lao Tzu - original Chinese name Lao Zi (551-479 BCE), *Dao De Jing* (often translated to English as *Tao Te Ching*). The concept is from Chapter 3 and throughout the book. This quote is the author's interpretation expressed in English.

2. Huang Di (2698-2598 BCE), *Huang Di Nei Jing* (often translated to English as *The Medical Classic of the Yellow Emperor*). Authorship is attributed to Huang Di, the Yellow Emperor, who was the first emperor of China. This book is considered the foundation of traditional Chinese medicine.

3. Osho, Emotions: *Freedom from Anger, Jealousy and Fear* (Osho Media International, 2010). This is the author's own expression inspired by Osho's reference to the waves and the ocean.

4 EMBODIED AWARENESS DEEPENS CONNECTION WITH AUTHENTIC SELF

1. Shakespeare, Hamlet, Act 1 Scene 3, spoken by King Claudius's chief minister Polonius.

2. Merrian-Webster; retrieved from https://www.merriam-webster.com/dictionary/authentic

3. Oxford Dictionary on Lexico.com; retrieved from https://www.lexico.com/en/definition/authentic

4. Bill George, *Authentic Leadership* (Jossey-Bass, 2004). Except the direct quote, expressions here are paraphrased by author based on key points in Bill George's book.

5. Friedrich Nietzsche, *Thus Spoke Zarathustra* (originally written in the 1880s; Latest publishing by CreateSpace Independent Publishing Platform, 2018)

5 EMBODIED AWARENESS BOOSTS EMOTIONAL INTELLIGENCE

1. Egyptian proverb; retrieved from http://www.greatthoughtstreasury.com/author/egyptian-proverbs

2. Daniel Goleman, *What Makes a Leader?* (Harvard Business Review, January 2004); retrieved from https://hbr.org/2004/01/what-makes-a-leader?referral=00060. Also on HBR video based on the same article by Daniel Goleman; retrieved from https://hbr.org/video/5236216251001/what-makes-a-leader

3. Chris Dulewicz, Mike Young, Victor Dulewicz, *The Relevance of Emotional Intelligence for Leadership Performance* (Journal of General Management, 2008)

4. Antonio R. Damasio, Q&A captured by Manuela Lenzen in article *Feeling Our Emotions* (ScientificAmerican Mind 16,1: 14-15, April 2005); retrieved from https://www.scientificamerican.com/article/feeling-our-emotions/

5. This quote has been attributed to various people including President Theodore Roosevelt, Earl Nightingale, John Maxwell, etc. Retrieved from https://coloradocommunitymedia.com/stories/its-not-how-much-you-know-its-about-how-much-you-care,253742

6. Frederic Laloux, *Reinventing Organizations: A Guide to Creating Organizations Inspired by the Next Stage of Human Consciousness* (Nelson Parker, 2014)

7. Lauri Nummenmaa, Enrico Glerean, Riitta Hari, and Jari K. Hietanen, *Bodily Maps of Emotions* (PNAS / Proceedings of the National Academy of Sciences, January 2014); contributed by Riitta Hari (2013) and retrieved from https://doi.org/10.1073/pnas.1321664111

6 EMBODIED AWARENESS ENHANCES EXECUTIVE PRESENCE

1. Lao Tzu - original Chinese name Lao Zi (551-479 BCE), *Dao De Jing* (often translated to English as *Tao Te Ching*), Chapter 26. This quote is the author's interpretation expressed in English.

2. Resource, July/August,1990; retrieved from http://www.SermonIllustrations.com/A-Z/L/Lincoln.htm

3. Jack Welch, *Importance of Executive Presence* (video from Jack Welch Management Institute, September 2019); retrieved from https://www.youtube.com/watch?v=VvqeKcFANpE&feature=youtu.be

4. Amy Cuddy, *Presence: Bringing Your Boldest Self to Your Biggest Challenges* (Little, Brown Spark; 2018)

5. Dan Schawbel, *Amy Cuddy: How Leaders Can Be More Present In The Workplace* (Forbes, February 2016); retrieved from https://www.forbes.com/sites/danschawbel/2016/02/16/amy-cuddy-how-leaders-can-be-more-present-in-the-workplace/#4b92d4f9731c

6. Interpersonal Neurobiology or Relational Neurobiology is a field initially created by Dan J. Siegel, now with a wide array of support from professionals and authors with books published as part of Norton Publishing's Series on Interpersonal Neurobiology (50+ books). Interpersonal Neurobiology (IPNB) is primarily a theory and practical working model which describes human development and functioning as being a product of the relationship between the body, mind and relationships. This expression is from Tim Clinton and Gary Sibcy's article *Christian Counseling, Interpersonal Neurobiology, and the Future* (Journal of Psychology and Theology, June 2012); retrieved from https://en.wikipedia.org/wiki/Interpersonal_neurobiology.

7. Emotional Contagion is a well-studied phenomenon by various scholars and researchers; Retrieved from https://en.wikipedia.org/wiki/Emotional_contagion#:~:text=Emotional%20contagion%20is%20the%20 phenomenon,ways%20both%20implicitly%20or%20explicitly.

8. Wendy Palmer, Janet Crawford, *Leadership Embodiment: How the Way We Sit and Stand Can Change the Way We Think and Speak* (CreateSpace Independent Publishing Platforms, 2013)

7 EMBODIED AWARENESS SUPPORTS LEADING CHANGE

1. This quote is most consistently attributed to Heraclitus (c. 535 BC – 475 BC), known for his doctrine of change being central to the universe.

2. Nitin Nohria, Michael Beer, *Cracking the Code of Change* (Harvard Business Review, May-June 2000); retrieved from https://www.google.com/amp/s/hbr.org/amp/2000/05/cracking-the-code-of-change

3. Ron Ashkenas, *Change Management Needs to Change* (Harvard Business Review, April 2013); retrieved from https://hbr.org/2013/04/change-management-needs-to-cha

4. A.J. Jacobs, Brief But Spectacular video series (PBS NewsHour, April 2016); retrieved from https://youtu.be/Shpfof68-zY

5. Carl G. Jung, referenced by Neel Burton M.D. in his article *Jung: The Man and His Symbols* (Psychology Today, April 08, 2012); retrieved from https://www.google.com/amp/s/www.psychologytoday.com/us/blog/hide-and-seek/201204/jung-the-man-and-his-symbols%3famp

8 INTRODUCTION TO DOING

1. Aristotle (384–322 BC), Greek philosopher. This version of English expression was first written by Will Durant, *The Story of Philosophy: The Lives and Opinions of the Greater Philosophers* (Simon & Schuster, 1926); retrieved from https://www.google.com/amp/s/medium.com/amp/p/66356f22843d

2. Michael Beer, Magnus Finnström, Derek Schrader, *Why Leadership Training Fails—and What to Do About It* (Harvard Business Review, October 2016); retrieved from https://hbr.org/2016/10/why-leadership-training-fails-and-what-to-do-about-it

3. Matt Plummer, Jo Wilson, *Become a More Productive Learner* (Harvard Business Review, June 2018); retrieved from https://hbr.org/2018/06/become-a-more-productive-learner. Original data quoted in this article is published by Association for Talent Development, in the article *Ensuring Learning Transfer* by Roy Pollock and Andrew Jefferson; available https://www.td.org/newsletters/atd-links/ensuring-learning-transfer

4. Matt Symonds, *Executive coaching - another set of clothes for the Emperor?* (Forbes, January 2011); retrieved from https://www.forbes.com/sites/mattsymonds/2011/01/21/executive-coaching-another-set-of-clothes-for-the-emperor/#5b425b4b118b

5. Wendy Palmer, Janet Crawford, *Leadership Embodiment: How the Way We Sit and Stand Can Change the Way We Think and Speak* (CreateSpace Independent Publishing Platforms, 2013)

6. Doug Silsbee, *Presence-Based Coaching: Cultivating Self-Generative Leaders Through Mind, Body, and Heart* (Jossey-Bass, 2008)

7. "The issues are in the tissues" is a well-referenced expression in the space of trauma and physical health. In the context of personal development and self-cultivation, the expression "the issue is in the tissue" can be traced to ancient wisdom practiced by energy practitioners such as Qigong master Mingtong Gu in video The Issue is In the Tissue (2019); retrieved from https://www.youtube.com/watch?v=bszC1FGfZe0. This expression has also been attributed to somatic educator Patrice Hamilton, as quoted by Michael Clemmens in his book *Embodied Relational Gestalt: Theories and Applications* (Gestalt Press, 2019)

9 EMBODIED ACTIONS TRANSFORM IMPULSE CONTROL

1. Epictetus (c. 50 – 135 AD), Greek philosopher; retrieved from https://www.quotenova.net/authors/epictetus/xawp6b

2. Daniel Goleman, *What Makes a Leader?* (Harvard Business Review, January 2004);

retrieved from https://hbr.org/2004/01/what-makes-a-leader?referral=00060. Also on HBR video based on the same article by Daniel Goleman; retrieved from https://hbr.org/video/5236216251001/what-makes-a-leader

3. Chris Dulewicz, Mike Young, Victor Dulewicz, *The Relevance of Emotional Intelligence for Leadership Performance* (Journal of General Management, 2008)

4. Daniel Goleman, *Self-Regulation: A Star Leader's Secret Weapon* (Daniel Goleman's website, July 2015); retrieved from http://www.danielgoleman.info/daniel-goleman-self-regulation-a-star-leaders-secret-weapon/

5. The Body-Centered Coaching training the author attended was created by Marlena Field, offered by MentorCoach LLC and delivered by instructor Pat Hinton Walker.

6. Viktor E. Frankl, *Man's Search for Meaning* (Beacon Press, 2006)

7. Daniel Goleman, *Emotional Intelligence: Why It Can Matter More Than IQ* (Bantam Books, 1995)

8. Antonio R. Damasio, Q&A captured by Manuela Lenzen in article *Feeling Our Emotions* (ScientificAmerican Mind 16,1, 14-15, April 2005); retrieved from https://www.scientificamerican.com/article/feeling-our-emotions/

10 EMBODIED ACTIONS ENABLE POWERFUL LISTENING

1. Lao Tzu - original Chinese name Lao Zi (551-479 BCE), *Dao De Jing* (often translated to English as *Tao Te Ching*). Chapter 66. This quote is the author's interpretation expressed in English.

2. Stephen R. Covey, *The 7 Habits of Highly Effective People* (Simon & Schuster, 1989)

3. Kenneth Blanchard, Spencer Johnson, *The One Minute Manager* (William Morrow & Co, Inc, 1982)

4. Michael Papay, Kate Benediktsson, *The Power of Listening: What It Means and Why It Matters* (Huffington Post, October 2016); retrieved from https://www.huffpost.com/entry/the-power-of-listening-what-it-means-and-why-it-matters_b_58129614e4b08301d33e079b

5. Donald O. Hebb, *The Organization of Behavior: A Neuropsychological Theory* (Psychology Press, 2002)

6. Amanda Blake, *Your Body Is Your Brain: Leverage Your Somatic Intelligence to Find Purpose, Build Resilience, Deepen Relationships and Lead More Powerfully* (Embright, 2019)

11 EMBODIED ACTIONS FACILITATE THINKING & ACTING STRATEGICALLY

1. This Chinese proverb is attributed to Wang Chong (AD 27-97) in his book *Lun Heng.*

2. Dorie Clark, *If Strategy Is So Important, Why Don't We Make Time for It?* (Harvard Business Review, June 2018); retrieved from https://hbr.org/2018/06/if-strategy-is-so-important-why-dont-we-make-time-for-it

3. Rich Horwath, *The Strategic Thinking Manifesto*; retrieved from https://www.strategyskills.com/pdf/The-Strategic-Thinking-Manifesto.pdf?gclid=ClaV2fG0v88CFcVlfgodSBUM8A

4. Donald O. Hebb, *The Organization of Behavior: A Neuropsychological Theory* (Psychology Press, 2002)

12 EMBODIED ACTIONS MAKE DELEGATION REAL

1. Lao Tzu - original Chinese name Lao Zi (551-479 BCE), *Dao De Jing* (often translated to English as *Tao Te Ching*). Chapter 38. This quote is the author's interpretation expressed in English.

2. Jack Welch, *Winning* (HarperLuxe, 2005)

3. Marshall Goldsmith, *What Got You Here Won't Get You There: How Successful People Become Even More Successful* (Hachette Books, 2007)

4. Daniel J. Siegel, *Pocket Guide to Interpersonal Neurobiology: An Integrative Handbook of the Mind* (W.W. Norton & Company, 2012)

5. Donald O. Hebb, *The Organization of Behavior: A Neuropsychological Theory* (Psychology Press, 2002)

6. A.J. Jacobs, *Brief But Spectacular* video series (PBS NewsHour, April 2016); retrieved from https://youtu.be/Shpfof68-zY

INVITATION

1. This quote is attributed to Audrey Hepburn; retrieved from https://www.goodreads.com/quotes/12732-nothing-is-impossible-the-word-itself-says-i-m-possible. Audrey Hepburn is also the author's favorite actress.

ABOUT THE AUTHOR

Yan Maschke is a strategy and leadership advisor and the founder of Yan Maschke Group. She works with corporate executives and leadership teams to elevate their impact through executive coaching, team coaching, and strategic facilitation. Clients often come to Yan for support on strategic thinking, team effectiveness, executive presence, and emotional intelligence.

Yan grew up in China and immigrated to the United States as a young adult. She spent most of her career leading strategy and execution with global cross-functional teams in Fortune 500 environments. Her work is informed by extensive experience in business P&L management, strategy, team development, and functional leadership. Her integrative leadership approach draws from the modern, the ancient, and life-long self-cultivation.

Yan earned an M.B.A. from Michigan State University and an M.A. in International Relations from University of Northern Iowa. She is credentialed as a Professional Certified Coach (PCC) by International Coaching Federation (ICF) and she received the President's Award from ICF Cleveland Chapter. Two of her client coaching stories have been featured by ICF as part of its *#ExperienceCoaching* global curation. Yan publishes a leadership blog at www.yanmaschke.com/blog.

Yan loves to travel and enjoys dancing, qigong, and yoga.

For more information:
www.YanMaschke.com